Watch the Ball
Bend Your Knees
That'll Be
$20 Please!

Ed Collins

Foreword by Billie Jean King

CAROLINE HOUSE BOOKS
Green Hill Publishers, Inc.
Ottawa, Illinois

Second Printing

Copyright © 1977 by E. S. Collins

All rights reserved, including the
right to reproduce this book, or
parts thereof, in any form,
except for inclusion of brief
quotations in a review.

ISBN: 0-916054-50-0
Library of Congress Catalogue Card Number 76-55626

Manufactured in the United States of America

Caroline House Books/Green Hill Publishers, Inc., Ottawa, Illinois 61350

"This book represents some of the soundest
teaching of any textbook on tennis."

— Dennis Van der Meer

Table of Contents *by subject*

Table of Contents *by order*

Foreword

Many people have asked me to write the foreword for their book. Although I feel honored, I decline most requests unless I am sure the book makes a unique contribution to the industry.

I have no qualms about the contribution Ed Collins' book will make to the tennis industry. Since the day Ed and his wife Judy stopped by our tennis camp in Lake Tahoe Nevada, seven years ago, I have followed their careers with interest. Ed spent two years teaching with the best tennis professional in the world, Dennis Van der Meer. Judy worked on layouts and graphics for our publications. Both are talented artists in their own right, having more than a flair for painting and interior design.

Since then, Ed has learned and implemented the best in modern tennis teaching techniques.

The Ed Collins Tennis College in San Diego is widely known as one of the most successful programs in the country, and his newspaper column and magazine articles regularly instruct thousands of tennis buffs.

His innovative methods will make it easier for you to learn tennis or improve particular segments of your game. As Ed lectures, the key is to learn tennis in a logical progression. Don't try to imitate the pros by slugging the ball. Slow down and keep it in the court. By following the guidelines Ed sets out in this book, I guarantee you will have more success and more fun.

Billie Jean King

Preface: (1) The Book

My intention is that you use this book as you would a weekly tennis lesson. Each article covers one facet or step in learning tennis. Each article prescribes a practice drill which will help you improve — if you devote sufficient time to it.

Be patient in learning. Try not to digest more than one thing at a time. It'll take you a month to learn some lessons. Read and re-read the article. Research the topic. Ask your coach or pro questions about it. Think about the topic several times a day. Overlearn it.

I have attempted to organize the lessons in a progressive series. It is conceivable the book could assist the beginner in learning to play — week by week. If you already know how to play, and would rather devote your time to one area, find it under the Table of Contents, by subject.

(2) The Method

Tennis is learned most effectively if you appreciate the various stages of play. It is almost impossible to master this game by emulating the pros; you can, however, learn to play tennis quickly if you understand and respect its difficulty.

Instead of trying to hit the serve 100 mph, it's more practical to hit it 30 mph and watch it go in. The suggestion is to experience the proper technique while you gradually increase the speed. Every stroke and tactic is learned in logical sequence — a *progression*.

The often repeated message in this book is to slow down. You are encouraged to experience tennis with rhythm, poise and balance. By hitting softly you'll have a better chance to unclench your grip, relax your arm, and feel the ball on the racquet. The longer it stays on the strings the more control you have over it. All this is possible if you adhere to the fundamentals.

The difference between an experienced tournament player and a flailing beginner is most obvious when evaluating their fundamentals. It's not that the advanced player can hit the ball harder, or skim the net lower, or hit corners, or make the ball dip and hop with spins; the reason he's good is because he doesn't miss so often. And the reason he doesn't miss so often is because he can control his muscles. His footwork is sound; he reacts early to the ball; his technique is conservative; his balance is excellent; and he hits the ball only as hard as he can control it. He is fundamentally strong.

Many of the drills take place within a small hitting area. You will learn to play *Shortcut* — a game played within the service lines. By decreasing the hitting area you will be forced to conserve your backswing and slow down. This will help develop the feel of stroking, rather than hitting the ball. After moving back to the baseline you'll experience a spacious freedom you never knew existed.

The success you have using this book is dependent on your attitude when playing and practicing. Tennis gives you many opportunities to fail. Almost every point ends with someone making a mistake. It's how you deal with these mistakes that determines your chances of becoming a player.

You can react to a mistake in one of two ways: positively or negatively. If you get mad, the chances of duplicating your error on the next shot are much greater than if you react positively. The objective is to learn from your mistakes, not brood over them. It's not always easy to do — you may have to practice.

The Method has evolved by continuously experimenting with our program and students. Over 8,000 tennis players attended our clinics at the Rancho Bernardo Tennis College in San Diego. Hundreds of tennis teachers and coaches have experienced our teaching techniques and progressions at annual tennis teacher workshops coordinated through the University of California at San Diego.

And the Method continues to evolve. At the present time we are conducting our resort clinic program — *Ed Collins' Tennis College* — at Winners Circle lodge in Del Mar, California. We stage semi-annual clinics at the Ken-Caryl Ranch in Denver, Colorado, we offer weekly instruction at a number of California locations, and this summer we'll hold the 4th annual *Ed Collins Summer Camp* for juniors. With all this tennis learning activity, we're bound to discover new and better ways of making a difficult game easier to learn.

(Continued)

(3) It's A Great Game

To all you non tennis players: Even though it's hard enough to get a court nowadays, I invite you to learn tennis and share in all the reasons it is such a great game.

First of all, it's a game. Everyone needs to do something other than work.

Probably the most important reason to play tennis, or any sport, is because it motivates you to take pride in your body. Running around in little white shorts is embarrassing if your belly sticks out. For that reason, tennis players usually push themselves away from the dinner table often enough so they'll at least "look good."

Tennis is a natural way to meet others who share a common interest. How else can you get together with someone you've recently met and want to see again? After a couple of sets you're on your way to cultivating a new friendship.

Tennis is a good family game, one which can give you and yours a reason to get together (or if you prefer, a game which periodically gets you out of the house for awhile).

Although tennis players usually make poor spectators (they'd rather be playing), it's fun occasionally to study the top players in ac-

IT'S A GREAT GAME!

tion. As your knowledge of the game grows, so does your appreciation. Watching and analyzing the pros becomes a hobby within a hobby.

After developing a semi-consistent forehand, backhand and serve, maybe you'll want to test your skills in a tournament. While many people play tennis for reasons other than competition (they get enough of that at work), many thrive on it. They seek out singles and doubles leagues, challenge ladders and tournaments.

And you don't have to be "good" to play in a tournament. If you consider yourself a hacker, find out how to enter the "D" or "C" division. You'll end up across the net with someone whose backhand is as "good" as yours.

On the court, tennis will offer you the greatest physical challenge you've ever faced. It's like chess: the more you learn, the more you'll discover you don't know. Although there are only a half-dozen strokes, there are literally hundreds of different shots to master. Even a Jimmy Connors will retire someday without learning many of them.

The perfect execution of these shots should be every player's goal on every shot. Hitting the ball in the sweet-spot of the racquet, past the outstretched arms of your opponent, is one of the exhilarating thrills in tennis — one which you don't forget for a week.

A tennis game (forehands, backhands, serves and volleys) is as tangible as a piece of art. It is yours to keep and take pride in. Through tennis you can satisfy your creative instincts — by building a game, developing a plan, and executing it in a match. The result produces a great sense of accomplishment.

For all these reasons, and a few more space prohibits, tennis is one of the most important things in many people's lives. It's a great game, and much more than that. Get yourself a racquet!

(4) The Thanks

Thanks to Jean Bellon, Frank Chaboudy, Alan Cheesebro, Teri Clavell, Judy Collins, Dave Dollins, Mike Donscheski, Al Hopp, Mark Jensen, Scott Leckman, Liane Marquez, Lucy Means, Scott McCarthy, Dophie Poiset, Gary Quandt, Dave Rapp, Anita Schwartz, Ruby Shamsky, Carlton Smith and Mike Vander Griend for your devoted work and friendship.

And special thanks to Jack Boyl, for without your ridiculous pen, many people would not "read" this book.

ED COLLINS
October, 1977

The Evolution of a Tennis Game

In tennis, everyone's in a hurry to get great. The courts are filled with nervous players, all trying to imitate the styles of Borg, Nastase, Connors and Evert.

Great strokes don't just happen — they evolve. When you see one of the pros hit an incredible crosscourt topspin forehand, you must realize it has taken him years of practice to develop that particular shot.

Don't try to imitate him. That's like trying to imitate a trapeze artist.

Tennis is learned and enjoyed best when the student appreciates the various levels and stages of development.

The first is called the *hit and giggle* stage. This is where the beginner hits some and misses some. He spends most of his time practicing against the backboard and playing *Mini Tennis* — simple rally games from a shortened hitting area, near the net. His objective is to have fun and learn about the bounce and spin of the ball.

14

A couple of months later the second stage begins — the *3-stroke game*. The player seeks instruction to improve his forehand, backhand and serve. He practices *shortcourt* from inside the service lines, and spends an equal amount of time working on each stroke. He learns to rally from the baseline. His blisters turn to calluses.

The third stage is called *Mountain Tennis*. As the student gets semi-serious about competition, one strategy governs his budding game — hit the ball over the net — high. His arching groundstrokes take the shape of little mountains. He decides to throw his racquet press away.

After wearing out a couple of pairs of tennis shoes, the player discovers he can direct his groundstrokes. He is in the *hit 'em where they ain't* stage. He learns to attack the backhand and hit cross-court. The rallies become longer as the player develops his patience and control of the ball. He's a player.

The fifth stage is the longest and most important. It lasts as long as it takes the player to average three hits each point. It's not easy.

A *three-hit* player has usually played at least three full years and is very respectable. He learns to use ball rotation to control the pace and shape of the ball.

Stage No. 6 is when the player begins to take advantage of the short ball and approaches the net. He's very selective, making sure he only comes in on the right ball. He spends time working on his net game. His spin serve begins to take shape.

The seventh stage is when the player starts to be clever. He varies the pace and spin of the ball. His groundstrokes develop pace and depth. His shots have more topspin and angle. He learns to use the entire court. He wins the club tournament and builds a trophy case in his den.

Many years later, the eighth stage is spent developing a more powerful and effective serve. The ranking tournament player follows his serve into the net, makes very few unforced errors, and develops a couple of tennis weapons. His game has a personality and people stop to watch him play. He's a star!

Avoid the 5 Most Common Mistakes in Tennis

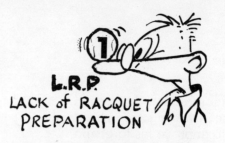

L.R.P.
LACK of RACQUET PREPARATION

HITTING OFF-BALANCE ②

SLOPPY FOOTWORK ③

OVER HITTING the BALL ④

LACK of RESTRAINT and CONCENTRATION ⑤

Your lifelong objective in tennis should be to avoid the following mistakes.

1. **Late racquet preparation.** The answer to smooth stroking is getting the racquet back in time. This will keep you from rushing your swing, which will prevent you from hitting the ball late, which will stop you from missing, which will put an end to your losing.

The racquet must be prepared before the ball crosses the net. In practice, say "Racquet back!" as soon as you decide which stroke to use; then start counting, "One thousand and one, one thousand and two, one thousand and . . ." If you can regularly make it to 1002 you are doing fine.

2. **Hitting off balance.** Hitting a moving tennis ball squarely in the middle of a little racquet is a tough task if you are moving also. Something has to be stationary.

Try being flat-footed at the crucial point of contact. Pretend you're a statue. Flex your front knee to absorb the shock of stopping suddenly. Keep the knee bent until the ball is gone. Don't move your head either; watch the spot where you made contact with the ball.

3. **Artless footwork.** Once the point starts, start moving, and don't stop until it ends. Keep a continuous rhythm to your footwork. Move quickly to the ball, taking many small adjustment steps, then slide back into position, bouncing gently on your toes until your opponent makes contact with the ball. Move back from the bounce so you play the ball as it descends. Be fluid.

4. **Overhitting.** Hit only as hard as you can control the ball. In every playing situation know what your objective is, what your tactics are, and how to execute them. Place a premium on control and depth. Aim high in baseline rallies and low when your opponent is at mid-court. Lob more and get your first serve in. Play intelligent tennis.

5. **Poor concentration.** Tennis is like chess. It takes the same kind of patience and concentration to become a respected player. Some points may take a dozen shots to evolve. The good player can restrain himself at the baseline and wait for the proper opportunity to try for a winner. If it doesn't present itself, he'll win the point by not missing.

BEGINNERS: Come to Grips With Your Racquet

The racquet is not a club — you shouldn't hold it like one.

If you're a sometimes-Sunday-afternoon-happy-hacker, let's get one thing straight about this game — the grips.

There are three: one for forehands, one for backhands and one for serves.

You can find the forehand grip by first holding the throat of the racquet in your left hand; place the palm of your right hand (right handers) flush against the strings; slide your hand down the handle, onto the grip and even with the butt of the racquet; spread your fingers diagonally up the handle, making sure there is a slight gap between your forefinger and middle finger. This is called the Eastern forehand, or "shakehands" grip.

To locate the backhand grip, place the palm of your hand on top of the racquet handle; the base-knuckle of your forefinger should line up with the outside bevel of the handle; wrap your thumb around the handle until it touches your middle finger. (Note: Make sure you do not point your thumb straight up the handle, no matter how uncomfortable it feels.) Again, spread your fingers.

The third grip is used by most players for serving. It is found by compromising between the forehand and backhand grips. The palm of the hand is placed on the top right bevel of the handle. This grip facilitates the proper use of the wrist.

When first learning to play, the grips are a big nuisance. It's difficult to see how they make a difference. But they do.

Develop the good habit of changing grips properly. Occasionally practice against a backboard, alternating backhands and forehands, changing grips each time.

Many intermediate-level players are plagued with erratic forehands because of using a "Continental" grip. After playing a backhand they never get their hand back to the other side of the handle. In their frustrated attempts to hit topspin they scatter the ball all over the court.

The most practical lesson in gripping the racquet is not to. Hold it lightly in your fingers, squeezing it gently only at the point of contact. In between shots, open your fingers so the grip can breathe.

(Among other things, squeezing the racquet causes blisters, bursitis, tennis elbow, net balls, out balls, lost balls, headaches and acne.)

"Shortcourt" (aka "Mini Tennis"): How and Why to Play It

It's painful to watch novice tennis players in their numerous attempts to get a rally going.

One hits it, the other chases it, one misses it completely, the other hits it into the net . . .

Occasionally they meet at the net to gather balls, each giving the other a look that says, "Why don't you hit it to me?"

If you're among the millions of struggling players who spend 95% of your time picking up balls and apologizing to your neighboring players for being a nuisance, then read and heed the following message.

Before you can expect to play a game of full-court tennis, like the experienced players, first master a lead-up game called "Shortcourt."

This is a groundstroke game (forehands and backhands) played within the boundaries of the service court.

With your partner, stand on opposite sides of the net at the service lines. Either player may start the point by dropping the ball and tapping it across the net and into the proper court. The point is in play only when the receiver successfully returns the ball. No volleying. Keep score ping-pong style; first to 15 wins.

The main purpose of this game is to have instant success. The shorter boundaries require that you slow down and attempt to control the

ball. The softer hit and the lower bounce make it possible for the beginner (and especially the "spaz") to enjoy a rally immediately.

In addition to the obvious satisfaction of being able to control the ball, "Shortcourt" helps the neophyte learn how to control the ball, to relax and be comfortable with the ball.

And because of the tremendous resiliency of ball and racquet, this is a lesson we can all benefit from. Instead of hitting at the ball, watching it ricochet unpredictably off the racquet, the serious student hits through the ball.

By moving closer to the net, slowing down, relaxing your arm, and following through on your strokes, you make it possible to develop a "feel" for the game. The ball stays on the racquet strings longer and you experience a sensation that you are motivated to reproduce again and again. And again.

And again.

THE NUMBER ONE FUNDAMENTAL:

BALANCE

When things are going poorly on the court, and nothing seems to work, it's probably time to go back to the basics.

Although everyone would like to think there's a subtle, magical secret to this game, that so far has escaped them — that as soon as they discover it they'll be on the road to fame, happiness and endless 6-0 sets — the fact is, to be a better tennis player you have to master the fundamentals.

And probably the most important fundamental is balance.

Balance makes it possible to improve your hand-eye coordination. In other words, it gives you a better chance to hit the ball in the center of the racquet.

Tennis is a game of precision: hitting a moving ball in the sweet-spot of the strings is no small task. It's even harder when the player is also moving.

Something has to be stationary.

You.

Being balanced at the point of contact is more likely if you step forward into the stroke, and this is possible only if you get to the ball early.

Anticipation and quick footwork are necessary skills.

When your opponent is making contact with the ball, you should be facing the net, feet spread, knees slightly bent, bouncing lightly on your toes.

Move quickly to the ball, taking small adjustment steps before striding forward into the stroke.

Bend your front knee with that stride. Get your foot flat on the ground. Turn your head so you are looking directly at the ball.

Stay down throughout the hit. Keep your foot flat, knee bent, head turned, until the ball has left your racquet. (If you pull up prematurely, you'll either mis-hit the ball or send it short.)

In practice, test your footwork and balance. Try holding your followthrough position, motionless, until the ball bounces on the other side of the net.

Continually challenge yourself to see how far you can move, how fast you can run, how quickly you can stop, and still maintain your balance.

Anticipate, move quick, stop, step forward, stroke the ball, stay down, and slide back into position.

Do all this and note the positive results you get. (Maybe balance *is* the secret.)

FOOTWORK:
MOVE FORWARD TO MOVE BACK

The ideal spot to hit forehands and backhands is waist-high, in front of the body.

It's here where tennis players have potential for both power and control (two characteristics that usually are not complementary).

Also, if you can step forward into the stroke, your chances of hitting an authoritative placement increase even more.

HOW TO FEEL
THE BALL
ON THE RACQUET

It all depends on your feet.

They determine whether you will be in the correct position, relative to the ball's bounce, to hit it properly.

The lesson here is to position yourself behind the ball's bounce, so you play the ball as it descends. (For most inexperienced and intermediate players this will be much easier than playing the ball on the rise.)

You have to move back quickly so you can move forward. Immediately turn sideways, take your racquet back, and get moving.

If you still find yourself contacting the ball too high and too late, then try a daily session of jump-roping.

This will make you a little bit stronger and psychologically a whole lot faster. You'll feel light-footed — and as you think, you are.

Good footwork is the basis of sound strokes and a healthy game. "Move back to move forward."

HOW TO FEEL THE BALL ON THE RACQUET

Good players seem to have nerves running into the grip, up the racquet handle, and through the strings.

They feel the ball. They are sensitive to where it hits on the racquet. They find the "sweet-spot" over and over again.

So can you.

Here's how:

1.) Never touch the ball with your free hand until you've first controlled it with the racquet. When someone tosses a ball for you to serve, stop its flight and control it completely before grabbing it. Also, if the ball is rolling or lying on the court, figure a way to pick it up with the racquet.

2.) Use the correct grips. Slightly spread your fingers up the racquet, making sure you have a space between your forefinger and middlefinger.

3.) Occasionally practice bouncing the ball down from waist height without mishitting the ball. Be deliberate and sensitive to center-hits.

4.) Practice the point-of-contact drill against a back-board. Stand 10 feet away, gently tapping the ball against the board. Take no backswing and limit your followthrough. Hit it in front of your body. Relax your fingers so you can feel the ball on the strings.

5.) Play "Shortcourt" as a warm-up before a match. Rally within the service lines in slow-motion, feeling the ball linger on the strings.

6.) Get away from the ball. The racquet is 27 inches long. When practicing against the backboard, playing "Shortcourt," or rallying from the baseline, make a special effort to keep your distance from the ball. Take small adjustment steps in your footwork so you have plenty of room to swing free and easy.

7.) Practice not missing. During the warm-up and in a point, concentrate on being smooth, graceful and on balance. Use long slow strokes to control the direction and pace of the ball. *Feel* your every move and hit.

8.) Play a lot. The more you play — the longer you hold the racquet in your hand — the more it becomes an extension of your arm. Someday you'll think you have strings between your fingers.

HOW TO KEEP YOUR FOREHAND INSIDE THE FENCES

A well hit, authoritative forehand can turn your life around.

It'll impress your friends and earn respect from your enemies. It'll make you a hero in your weekly doubles match. It'll give you gobs of self-confidence in singles. It'll give your whole game a personality.

All you have to do is learn how to hit it.

You may recognize that when your forehand is disobeying your elbow flies up as the ball flies out. On the followthrough you notice your elbow hanging disjointedly from your side. Why?

It may be your grip. If you are unwittingly trying to use a Continental grip (between a forehand and backhand), and you haven't been playing too long, you may be disappointed in your results. Try using an Eastern forehand grip: the V formed by the thumb and forefinger lies directly over the top of the racquet handle; the palm of your hand is flush against the side panel of the racquet.

Check your wrist too. Sometimes the obnoxious thing will keep you from enjoying a consistent forehand. If there is too much play in it, you may have found the source of trouble.

The wrist position on the forehand should be layed back. To find out how, crouch down and put the palm of your hand flat on the ground; see the wrinkles on the back of your wrist. Lift your hand up without changing the position of your wrist, grip the racquet and assume the correct point of contact position. Notice how the wrist is layed back at the POC. Practice tapping 1000 balls against a backboard until you get the proper feel.

After you've familiarized yourself with the proper grip and wrist positions, practice your new trouble-free forehand. Hold your finish and make sure you have a clear view of your shot *over* the top of your elbow.

Get the racquet back early, start below the ball, keep your wrist layed back, hit the ball in front, and follow through high.

Now keep it in the court!

 KISS

WHAT IT MEANS TO YOUR TENNIS GAME

K.I.S.S. . . . In the Army it means "Keep It Simple, Stupid!"

KISS applies to your tennis game too. The most conservative technique is always the most effective.

Simplicity is the key. On the serve, it is simpler and more effective if you start with your weight back — instead of rocking back, then forward. If you extend your tossing arm straight up — instead of circling it — you'll improve your consistency. Also, by relaxing your upper torso and keeping your back straight — rather than arching underneath the ball — you will enjoy a greater percentage of first serves in the court. It's less complicated.

The forehand is the average player's biggest source of winners; unfortunately, it's an even bigger source of errors. If the player always yields to the temptation of crunching the ball, he'll never develop the consistency needed to beat the club champ. Instead of winding up like a discus thrower, it's more effective if the player consolidates his backswing on the forehand. The racquet head should be drawn back below the level of the player's head and not continue past a point which is perpendicular to the net. Simplified technique for steady success.

At the net, the exaggerated backswing will lead to many disappointing failures. It's wise to keep the backswing concise and on the ball. When hitting an overhead, the intelligent player draws the racquet straight back over his shoulder so he'll be ready to reach up and meet the ball in front.

Be a nice neat little package on the court. Prepare early, eliminate excessive use of the wrist, conserve your backswing and be on balance. KISS!

Respect the Progression

The real joy of tennis is controlling the ball and the person on the other side of the net. Hitting a decisive point-winning shot, after first surviving a long rally, is one of the most exhilarating thrills in sport.

To eventually experience that thrill it is necessary to respect the inherent difficulty of the game. Before you can learn to hit the ball hard (and expect it to go in) *you first must learn to hit it softly*.

Everyone wants to be a winner by hitting winners. When they finally do hit one they're totally surprised. Their gracious opponent acknowledges the play by saying, "Good shot." The player returns the acknowledgement with, "It was nothing. . . . I just closed my eyes and swung."

Many players have little idea where their shots will go. They hope they go over the net and into the green area somewhere. This explains why there are so many hot and cold players around. Everything is left to chance; skill has little to do with it.

Everyone can learn to play exhilarating tennis by following this three-step process:

1. Slow down. Hit the ball only as hard as you can control it. When you start surprising yourself, slow down a little.

2. Follow through. In order to direct the ball you have to keep it on the strings for a moment. There is a big difference between hitting and stroking a tennis ball: one lingers on the racquet and goes where you wish, the other doesn't stay long enough for you to tell it what to do. Make sure you hit "through" the ball. Long, linear strokes will make the ball respond to your every command.

3. Predetermine every shot. Even during practice have a plan for every ball you hit. Aim it somewhere. When warming up make every ball go to your opponent's forehand, then his backhand, then alternate. In a match, plan the pace and direction of every shot.

Eventually your skills and confidence will grow (progress) to the point where you'll be surprised when you miss a shot, rather than when you make one.

33

DON'T RUN AROUND YOUR BACKHAND!

One of the great American pastimes is running around the backhand.

Everyone does it. Even Bjorn Borg does it.

You shouldn't.

Until your backhand gets as good as your forehand, play a backhand with a backhand.

Sounds painful, huh? Risk all that embarrassment and frustration when you could be unleashing topspin forehands all over the place? I know it's tough medicine, but it's for your own good. After all, you're going to play tennis for many years to come, and if you someday want to play on the 'A' ladder, you'll have to develop a game without a glaring weakness, because at the top levels of play you'll only be as good as your poorest stroke.

So improve your backhand.

The first step is to get the proper mental image of what it looks like. Go to the courts and locate someone who makes the backhand look effortless. Spend a good half-hour watching the player. Don't take your eyes off him (or her). Forget the ball — just study the motion.

After you've had an eye-full, go to the local backboard and put into effect what you've seen.

The "secret" to effortless backhands is early racquet preparation (erp). Before bounc-

ing the ball down to hit it, bring your racquet back so your hand is resting against your left thigh.

Make contact with the racquet slightly tilted back, imparting (a little) underspin to the ball.

Stay sideways throughout the stroke; let only your arm do the work. On the follow-through, lift your arm up so you expose your armpit.

As you continue to rally against the board, let the ball bounce twice — so you have time to prepare the racquet (erp) and fol-lowthrough (armpit).

After a couple of practice sessions with the board, take your skills to the court.

As soon as you see the ball coming to your backhand, say "Erp!" When it bounces, say "Bounce." And when you follow through, say "Armpit."

That's "ERP . . . BOUNCE . . . ARMPIT." (But don't let anyone hear you.)

Simplifying Your Forehand

Beginners love the forehand. It's the only shot they can understand. It's almost like hitting a baseball — square off, racquet back and let 'er go! Instant success. Compared to the other strokes, it's a snap.

Somewhere during the evolution of a tennis player's game, the forehand often stops being so much fun. Maybe it's because the other strokes become easier to hit — even easier than the forehand. In comparison, the forehand becomes a complex assemblage of motor skills.

Occasionally the player develops into a "head case" — psychologically he makes the forehand more difficult than it is.

For you psyched-out sluggers, there are only two things you have to remember about the forehand stroke: the beginning and the end. Two positions — that's it.

The first position to establish in your mind is the pivot position. As soon as determining you will play the approaching ball with a forehand, pivot. From a ready position with both hands on the racquet, turn your shoulders so your left hand guides the racquet head around until it is facing the net. Your shoulders should automatically be perpendicular to the net, with the racquet head even with your right shoulder. Your weight is now balanced on your right foot, which pivots in the same direction as your racquet.

The second, and final position to learn is the followthrough. (This is where the racquet finishes as the stroke is completed.) Your hand should be at the level of your eyes. The racquet handle is vertical to the ground (like a telephone pole). Your hand should be directly in front of your left shoulder (you are looking over your forearm to see where the ball went). Your weight has shifted to your front foot and your front knee is slightly bent.

Practice in front of a mirror. Check your pivot and then the follow through. Don't worry about what comes in between. With most students this part takes care of itself.

When practicing on the court, remind yourself to pivot early. Say "pivot" as soon as you see the ball approaching. When the ball bounces, say "bounce." As you hit through the ball, remind yourself to "follow through" (say it). "Pivot . . . bounce . . . follow through." (There is a definite rhythm here — learn it.)

To check your balance and note your followthrough, try holding your finish position until the ball bounces on the other side of the net. Practice this drill a few hours and your simplified forehand will do you proud.

The Four Most Frequently Suggested Tennis Tips

You can pick up many valuable tennis tips by eavesdropping on your local pro giving a lesson.

"Racquet back! Watch the ball! Bend your knees! Follow through!"

"Racquet back! Watch the ball! Bend your knees! Follow through!"

"Racquet back! Watch the ball! Bend your knees! Follow through!"

It won't take long before you've heard it all.

That's because there isn't much to hear. Those four suggestions sum it up.

"Racquet back!" is a plea to get the student in a comfortable position to stroke the ball. Shoulders turn, the feet pivot, and the racquet is drawn back in anxious anticipation of the shot. This all must happen simultaneously, as soon as the player determines which stroke to use — forehand or backhand. Billie Jean King says that racquet preparation is more important than the execution of the shot.

"Watch the ball!" is a recommendation to concentrate and follow it up to the point of contact. During and immediately after contact, it is wise to keep your eyes down. This will help give you a better chance to make a center hit.

"Bend your knees!" is every coach's advice to be on balance. When you make contact with the ball your body must be in control so you can control the racquet head. This is easiest when hitting every ball with your front foot on the ground, knee bent, on balance.

"Follow through!" is a reminder to stroke the ball, rather than hit it. The longer it stays on the racquet the more control you have over its destiny. This is possible if you relax your arm and grip on the racquet. Even at the point of contact, stay loose so you can feel the ball.

"Racquet back! Watch the ball! Bend your knees! Follow through!"

Do it.

IMPROVE YOUR RHYTHM AND TIMING

To be a good tennis player it is necessary to experience the rhythm of the game.

Beginning players have problems developing natural timing on the court. Things become easier when the student learns how to talk to himself during the rally.

If you have trouble judging the bounce of the ball, the next time you practice talk to yourself as you hit. From the baseline, say *bounce* every time the ball bounces — and *hit* as it is hit. When you and your partner are both at the baseline you'll find there is quite a pause between bounces. You'll be pleasantly surprised to find the ball isn't on top of you as soon as you thought.

Don't rush your shots. Move back from the bounce of the ball, playing it as it descends. To get the feel of this rhythm, pause between the *bounce* and *hit* on your side. Say *bounce aaaannnnd hit*.

Even tournament players have trouble with their timing. When faced with a booming serve they occasionally get psyched out. They think the ball is coming at them faster than it is. This is also the case with intermediates playing at the net. They'll close their eyes and turn their head like a Little League catcher.

Try the same verbal timing-device. When the ball is hit (by the server or baseliner) say *hit* — and when you play it say *hit*. The obvious time lag will help you feel the rhythm, gain your poise, and play the ball. Try it.

Learn Something About Learning

It's no wonder everyone wants to learn tennis — it's such an appealing game. Playing a long controlled point, and ending it with a decisive winning shot appears to be an ecstatic experience.

Learning the sport is something else. To be a good player takes several years of conscientious effort. In the meantime, the game draws on every physical and mental skill imaginable.

Learning tennis is not fun; having learned is fun. If you are struggling to get past the frustrating beginning stages, it may help to know something about the learning process.

Step No. 1 is making a sincere self-commitment to learn. You have to want it. This is often difficult because there is much failure along

the way. You're bound to get discouraged. Some days you'll feel like a complete *spaz* — worse than the first day out. Don't
fret. The human being must learn to ride out
his biophysical curve. Sometimes you're up
and sometimes you're down. Even the pros
admit, "It just wasn't my day."

The best solution to these days of depression is to get remotivated. Watch a tennis
match on TV; read a tennis book or magazine;
take a lesson; enter a tournament, etc. Get
yourself psyched-up again.

Step No. 2 is bombarding your senses
with tennis stimuli. The most effective method
of learning is to open your eyes and take in all
the tennis you can. Spend as much time as
possible watching and listening to good tennis
(this is how you can learn the rhythm of the
game).

Try to be selective when spectating.
Watch smooth baseline players who do not
overhit the ball.

Step No. 3 is practicing mentally. After
creating the mental picture of good tennis,
practice it in your mind. Twice a day imagine
yourself playing a series of long controlled
points from the base line. Think about it.

Step No. 4 is active physical practice.
Repetition is learning. Spend at least three one-
hour sessions working on your game. With a
practice partner or against a backboard, dis-
cipline yourself to hit thousands of tennis balls.
Realize the main difference between you and
the club champ is that he has hit more balls
than you. Even though you understand the skill
intellectually, repeat it frequently so your
muscles won't forget. Overlearn it.

Step No. 5 is seeking qualified help. "If
you could see yourself as others see you. . . ."
Your objective is to learn the progression that
leads to a solid fundamental game. Unfortunately, the impatient learner wants to be
successful as he sees success. It doesn't work
that way. If you imitate the pros you'll never get
on the right track. Learn to play in a logical,
realistic style that will enable you to always
improve. Take lessons. Find out how to do it.

Step No. 6 is to always be positive on the
court. Tennis gives you much opportunity for
failure. For the first couple of years, nine out of
ten points will end with a mistake. Instead of
brooding over an error, learn from it. Never say
never. Always look forward to the next
challenging point.

Teach Yourself the Slice Backhand

I once met a tennis player whose backhand was so lousy that instead of trying to hit it, half the time he caught it with his free hand and gave up the point. I found out later he developed this habit from playing on a court situated next to a cliff.

The backhand shouldn't be such a struggle. At the tournament level of play the backhand is the easiest stroke. Why? Among several reasons, one is that most backhands by the better players are hit with a slice action; anatomically, it is a more natural and effortless way to hit the ball. You can learn this too. Follow the progression:

Choke up on your racquet and rally with a practice partner from inside the service lines. Bevel (tilt) the racquet face back slightly and tap the balls back and forth. No backswing! Notice the underspin you are creating; the ball is spinning backward as it crosses the net.

Keep your arm straight and restrain from chopping at the ball. The bevel of the racquet face will do the work for you. Practice for 15 minutes and see how many times you and your partner can consecutively keep the ball in play inside the service lines. Set a goal and reach it.

Now move back a few feet, gradually lengthening your backswing and follow-through. You may lower your grip an inch. Look for the backspin. It is important you follow through up — not down. Hit for another 10 minutes before moving back to the baseline.

From the baseline use the full stroke. Turn sideways. Remember: early racquet preparation is crucial, critical and important. Racquet back, shoulders closed, before the ball bounces in front of you.

Reach out far for the ball, slicing through as you make contact. Finish high. Your hand should end up at the level of your head. Air your armpit!

Be deliberate as you address the ball. If you slug it with the racquet face beveled back, you'll spend most of your time chasing stray balls. Underspin facilitates a defensive control shot — not a crunching winner. Don't be violent. Carefully slide through the ball and you'll be the proud possessor of a budding backhand. Congrats!

TWO-HANDED BACKHANDS ARE EASY TO HIT

In the continuing evolution of tennis styles and tactics, the most recent change involves the backhand.

Nowadays many players use two hands. Of the top 10 ranked male international stars, four hit their backhands with double-fisted grips; on the female side, almost every teenage tennis player is a disciple of Chris Evert.

The popularity of the two-handed stroke is due, in part, to early introduction of youngsters to tennis. Some are taught to walk and rally at the same time. Their infantile lack of strength makes it difficult to handle a backhand with one hand, so they grab hold with two. Later, after they develop the necessary forearm and grip strength to use one hand, they are too comfortable to change.

For these future Bjorn Borgs and Chris Everts, there are advantages and disadvantages in using two hands.

The obvious advantage is the power it adds to the stroke. It is beyond the ability of most to slug the backhand. With one hand, because of the backhand grip and the relative lack of strength, it's easier, and more effective, to slice the ball with underspin; however, with the support of two hands, the player can either hit it flat or lift the ball over the net with topspin. His stroke changes from a defensive control shot to an offensive weapon.

The disadvantage of using two hands is that it eliminates the extensive reach of the one-handed shots. On both wide and low balls the two-hander has trouble.

It appears that the great two-handed players of today make up for their lack of reach with anticipation and quickness afoot. Evert, Borg, Connors, Soloman and Dibbs are tenacious scramblers, whose mobility and court coverage are always a treat to watch.

If you've ever wondered if your backhand could benefit by the support of an extra hand, simply slide your free hand down so it touches the other — like gripping a baseball bat. The same principles of stroke production apply: draw the racquet back before the ball bounces, turn your shoulders, hit the ball in front, and follow through.

On the followthrough you have the choice of letting go with your left hand (for right handers) or holding on throughout the stroke. If you hold on, make sure you don't press too much with your second hand. Make sure the racquet finishes on a line with your right shoulder, and perpendicular to the ground. You should have a clear view of your shot over your left elbow. As you rally, hold this followthrough position momentarily while checking to see it's OK.

If the backhand has always been the main source of your tennis depression, you may discover that using two hands is good medicine.

"SHOW YOUR NUMBERS" ON THE BACKHAND

Failure to rotate the shoulders properly is the greatest single cause of a flailing backhand.

The *transfer of learning* concept partially explains why most players' backhands are a constant source of embarrassment. The inexperienced player, when hitting forehands, can succeed without first turning his shoulders to the side. Since strength is not crucial when hitting from an open (facing the net) stance, he has no problem. Later, when the player tries to learn the backhand, a negative transfer of learning occurs. He didn't have to rotate his shoulders on the forehand, so he doesn't worry about it on the backhand.

To overcome this learning dilemma, you'll have to work extra hard to develop the backhand technique — a technique that eventually will become a habit, and that habit will some day make your backhand a fun shot to hit.

Pretend you have numbers on the back of your shirt, like a baseball player. Whenever a ball approaches your backhand side, rotate your shoulders so your opponent can see your numbers. Do it as quickly as you see it's coming to the backhand. Before the ball bounces say to yourself, "Show my numbers." Make a game of it. For the next few weeks prepare for every backhand that way.

Once you *show your numbers* properly, the backhand is one of the most uncomplicated shots in the game. It's just your arm that does the work. Some liken the motion to that of throwing a frisbee. Stay sideways to the net throughout the entire stroke. Reach forward to make contact. Try to hit the ball as far out front as possible. Follow through high, so your hand is above eye level.

See? It's easier than you thought.

48

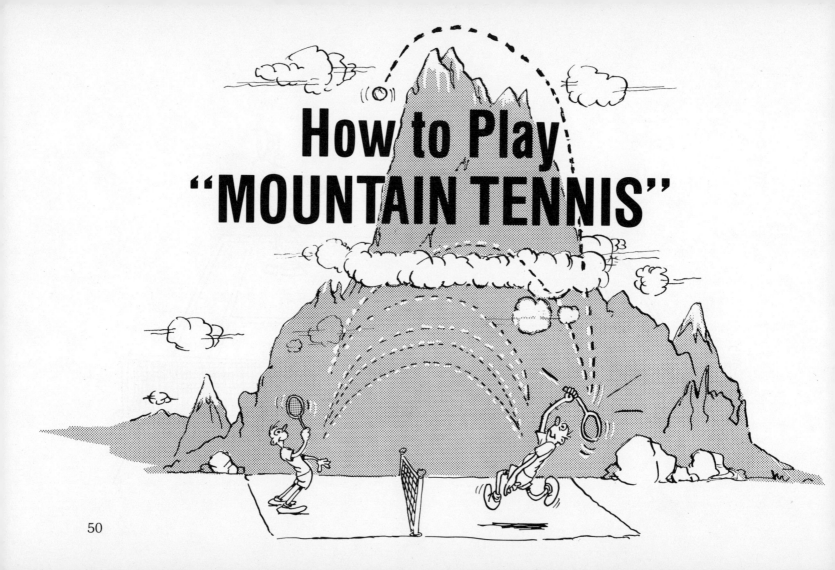

How to Play "MOUNTAIN TENNIS"

The most important strategy in tennis is exceedingly simple: HIT THE BALL OVER THE NET.

In spite of the simplicity of this *First Rule of Tennis*, players frequently break it. In fact, over 60 percent of point losing errors are made into the net.

The **worst** mistake you can make is to hit the ball short. Generally, this means you are trying to be too clever, skimming the net like the superstars (appear) to.

Many big-hitting intermediates can't clear the net by a safe margin because of the super-high velocity of their groundstrokes. If their drives pass over the net by more than a foot or two, the ball hits the fence. If you share this problem, slow down. If you cannot clear the net by four to six feet, you are hitting too hard.

The second **worst** way to terminate the point is to send the ball wide. This often indicates you are trying to be better than you are. If you have trouble directing the ball, aim down the center of the court.

The **best** way to end the point (if you have to make a mistake) is to hit the ball long. This is OK. You are heeding the baseline strategy of trying to keep the ball deep. After all, if you can make your opponent play the ball from behind the baseline, even Jimmy Connors won't be able to hit a winner. At least he shouldn't.

A healthy way to approach your mistakes in tennis is to evaluate whether they were consistent with your objective. If you make the mistake of hitting long, and your strategy was to keep the ball deep, you could say you made a **positive error.** If you hit the ball short, but were trying to keep it deep, you obviously made a negative error. Every percentage-tennis player's goal is to make as many positive errors as possible.

Do You Belong at the Net Yet?

Sam thought he was ready for the *serve and volley* game. He had been playing baseline tennis for six months — twice a week — a real weekend warrior.

"Now I'm ready to start putting the pressure on," Sam said. "I'll intimidate my opponents with deftly angled volleys and

charging the net at every opportunity possible. By slapping their feet on the court and beating their chest, they cause many excited opponents to suffer nervous breakdowns every time they stampede the net.

As long as you pick your opponents wisely, this crazy tactic will prove to be effective.

crunching overheads — just like Newcombe."

The first time Sam approached the net he had an accident. That experience has since left an indelible impression on Sam's mind (and his teeth). Sam is now a nervous tennis player.

Many players employ this scare tactic of net rushing. They intimidate their oponents by

If, however, you're up against a decent player, you will end up jogging back and forth from the net like a yo-yo.

Don't make the same mistake Sam did. Stay at the baseline and develop your groundstrokes. Otherwise, it may take you forever learning how to play.

TBAS:
The Secret to the Dinker's Success

Nobody likes a *dinker*. At a cocktail party nobody will talk to him. He's usually a loner — aloof. He's also the champ — *numero uno* on the ladder. You hate him!

How can you beat this player? You've tried everything and he always comes out on top. You've experimented with net rushing, hitting short balls, topspin, underspin, wide-angled shots, lobbing and drop shots. . . . Nothing works. He's invincible.

How can you beat 'em? You can't. In tennis you never beat anybody. They beat themselves. And that's how you must play the dinker. Give him an opportunity to beat himself.

The dinker is the champ only because he has a longer **tennis ball attention span.** *TBAS* is the amount of patience each player displays in his game. Some players' attention is good for two shots, some three, some four—some can hit eight balls in a row before getting impatient and making a nervous mistake. If you are going to be competitive with the Champ, you'll have to play like one.

Give the dinker an opportunity to demonstrate his TBAS. Pretend you are a *human backboard;* get everything back.

Try to move him around. Obviously, this can be accomplished only if you have the skills. (If you don't, then relax, taking your whipping in stride.) Can you hit a short angled underspin ball to his forehand and follow it up with a deep drive to his backhand? Now take a step into the court and anticipate a weak return.

It's tough to beat the dinker from the baseline. This is the playing situation where he feels the most comfortable. You must try to make him uncomfortable.

The dinker often sets up camp deep behind the baseline. Most players don't have the skills to drop-shot, so he doesn't concern himself with the short ball. This bit of info may prove helpful to us. If we can occasionally play a short underspin approach shot that bounces inside the service line, we may catch the dinker sleeping. He'll be forced to run in to play the short low ball. We can get close to the net and force him to hit the ball up. Then we can smash it down his throat! (Just kiddin'!)

From the net we have a wider angle with which to work. Again, it is imperative to have the necessary skills before venturing up there. For example, being at the net without an adequate overhead is like going hunting without ammunition. You won't scare anybody.

Remember — the dinker depends on your careless errors to get him through the battle. He doesn't have a weapon. His offense is a good defense. If you use your imagination and do not give him free points, you stand a better chance. At least you'll get a great workout. Have fun!

HOW TO SYNCHRONIZE YOUR SERVE

Is your tossing motion faster than your hitting motion, and is your toss so inconsistent that when you finally hit the ball your startled opponent yells, "Good get!"?

The source of your difficulty is probably your "unsynchronized start." If you toss the ball before taking your racquet back (or vice versa), you are losing rhythm, consistency and speed in your serve.

The following clues will help develop a synchronized start and fluid serve.

1. Start with both hands together. Hold the ball in your fingertips and rest the throat of the racquet on your thumb. Bend both elbows, pointing racquet in direction of court. Body weight is back.

2. Drop arms down together at same time. As you practice, say "down together." Transfer your weight forward to front foot.

3. Touch the inside of your left thigh with the ball before you start up with the tossing arm. Say "down together — touch."

4. Develop an "open face backswing." Immediately on the downswing, begin to "open" the face of the racquet. Rotate your palm so it is facing the net.

5. Bring both arms up together as you release the ball at the highest point possible. Don't toss it — release it so it doesn't spin. Say "up together."

6. As you practice the entire motion, talk to yourself. Say "down together . . . touch . . . up together." Say it slowly. (Remember that this part of the serve is slow; it's the end where you speed up.)

The Five Sources Of Power In Serving

Everybody wants one. Even if you can't play well, with a big serve you gain instant respect.

Developing a big serve is possible only if you develop the technique that makes it possible to have one. Where many go wrong is in trying to hit the serve hard by swinging harder. The ball goes faster, but not in.

The secret to a big serve is not swinging harder, but swinging easier. Rhythm and relaxation are the main ingredients in the power serve.

The first source of power is a proper weight transfer. The body's weight should move from the back to the front foot during the tossing motion. As you drop your hands down to start the tossing motion, slowly transfer your weight forward. Balance is important to a powerful serve, so keep it.

The second power source is a live, loose, relaxed arm. In order to achieve good racquet-head speed it is imperative the arm stays flaccid. The motion must be continuous, without hesitations or jerky movements. Be loose. You can monitor the tenseness of your arm by checking your grip as you begin the serve. Consciously keep it loose throughout the backswing. (To get the idea, hold on to only the butt-end of the racquet with two fingers and your thumb, then try your serve.)

The third source of power is proper timing. A sequence of events takes place in the serve that must be properly coordinated.

First event is the backswing and weight-transfer. From a ready position with your hands at the level of your chest, drop them down together slowly to begin the motion. Make this part of the serve very deliberate. Start slowly so you can finish fast.

The second sequence is a complete elbow bend. The racquet drops down behind the back as it coils for the upward spring. (To see if you're getting enough elbow flex, try serving a few, touching the small of your back before swinging up.)

The shoulder turn follows the elbow bend. The shoulders roll through to facilitate the upward movement of the elbow. (To check if you are coordinating this properly, hold your followthrough position to see if your right shoulder (for right handers) is lower than the left.)

The final source of power is the wrist snap. At the point of contact the racquet head is thrust upward and outward. (Hold the racquet in the middle and see if the butt rotates to the outside of your forearm.)

Keep your power serve under control. At the moment of impact try to keep your balance without falling into the court. If your body is out of control, so will be your serve. Keep your head steady with your eyes and chin up until after the ball leaves the racquet. Remember, you're hitting up, not down.

59

How to *(Realistically)* Practice This Game

Practice alone does not make perfect.

This may come as a shock if recently you've been spending long hours on the practice court, hitting forehands, backhands and volleys until your hand bleeds. All that rallying for nothing?

Not really. The point is that a great rallier does not make a great player.

On the other hand, by spending all your court time playing tournament and challenge matches, you never practice your weakness(es). You only do what is necessary to win.

There is a way to combine the benefits of practicing and competing.

The solution is to play "practice matches." Instead of playing to win, you play to practice.

Pick your weakest weakness. If it's your backhand, on your next tennis date talk your partner into playing "21" — a ground-stroke game without the serve. Each point begins with a backhand. The ball must be hit three times before the point begins. (This encourages you to start each point with a controlled rally.) Either player may start the rally. No net rushing. Score is kept Ping-Pong style: 1, 2, 3, 4, 5 . . . until someone reaches 21, with a margin of two. (A variation for advanced-level tennis is to penalize the player when his shot lands short of the service line.)

If you're a shy possessor of an embarrassing second serve, play "One Serve." Instead of two chances, you have only one to start the point. Structure the rules so you may not rush net, or drop shot, after the point begins. Stay back and work on your baseline game — remembering that a player is only as good as his ground strokes.

For you big serve-and-volleyers (advanced players with at least three years' tournament experience) play a practice game called "Half-speed." The simplified rules are:

1) the server must indicate to the receiver where he will direct his serve; 2) the server hits his serve at "half-speed," 3) the server must follow his serve into net; and 4) the receiver plays all returns down the middle of the court, at half-speed. After the return, anything goes.

The purpose of your practice sessions should be to strengthen a weakness. Try not to make the mistake of many players: their goal is to win — any way possible. When they lose, they prefer being beaten by a respectable score, like 6-4, rather than lose 6-2 and help their game.

Improving at something is everything. This is possible only if you leave your ego and fanatical will to win off the practice court. Consider your practice matches an opportunity to practice your tennis game. If you're having trouble with the backhand, stay back at the baseline and run around your forehand. Most people do just the opposite: they hide their weakness from everyone except themselves. Intermediates lack the experience to take advantage of a player's weakness, so they seldom are punished; advanced players, however, will uncover the weakness and expose it to the world.

POSITIVE MISTAKES:
How to Make 'Em

Have you noticed that mistakes on the court come in clusters? Usually they happen three at a time. Here's how you can learn to make only one at a time.

The clue is to only make *positive mistakes*; that's opposed to making *negative mistakes*.

If you make a dumb shot, you have the choice of looking at it one of two ways: you either bad-mouth yourself (". . . You big dummy!") or you positively reinforce the correct approach to the shot ("I could have done that better by . . .")

It has been said by physiologists that your muscles do not respond properly after negative mistakes. It takes approximately three shots to recover from such a mistake. Although you may successfully make the the next shot after one, your muscles won't get their *feel* back for three more shots.

Every player's objective is to make only positive mistakes. Each error must teach you something, reinforce something positive about the stroke which will make it possible to play the next one better (i.e., "Prepare faster next time, please.")

Another suggestion is always to compliment your opponent when he makes a nice shot. Don't get upset when he occasionally aces or passes you. That produces the same anxiety in your muscles that a negative mistake does.

Acknowledge his good shots as "good shots." You can even go so far as saying "Good shot!" when you make a questionable error. It's a psychological game you play with yourself — meant to keep you poised, confident and forever smiling.

Slow Down Racquet, Speed Up Feet

Play tennis with fast feet and a slow racquet.

Write that down on a piece of adhesive tape and put it on the side of your racquet. During your matches occasionally glance down and read what it says.

Make sure you read it carefully. Do not get it backwards; that's fast feet and a slow racquet — not slow feet and a fast racquet.

Many beginning and intermediate level players play a unique version of tennis that should be called *jungle ball*. In this game there are no long rallies, no footwork, no balance, no suspense, and no thinking. The only strategy is to wait until the ball comes, lay back and beat the heck out of it. Hopefully it'll go in the court.

Even though *jungle ball* is sometimes fun, you can increase your enjoyment of tennis by increasing the length of your points. This entails slowing the pace of your shots and improving your mobility so you get to more balls.

A *slow racquet* means you are hitting through the ball, rather than at it. The ball stays on the strings momentarily so you can influence its direction, speed and spin. If you slug, punch or slap at the ball, it will not linger on the strings long enough for you to maintain control. Where it goes after leaving the racquet is always a surprise.

Swinging a tennis racquet is analogous to swinging a baseball bat. In order to hit the baseball hard you have to swing easy. All the power in baseball, and tennis, come directly from the sweet spot. To find it, you'll need a smooth, steady, flowing swing — a slow racquet.

You'll also need a fast pair of feet. Maybe they don't have to be fast, just moving. Since most opponents try to hit the ball where you're not, you have to get to where it is. Then, when you get there, you have to be on balance so you can use your smooth, steady, flowing "sweet-spot" swing.

Take small steps. Stay on your toes. Spread your feet wide as you move. Bounce rhythmically when your opponent strikes the ball. Hit the ball with one foot flat on the court. Keep your front knee bent until the ball is gone. Slide immediately back into position. Be loose.

Remember — that's *fast* feet and a *slow* racquet.

THE WRIST SNAP— HOW TO PRACTICE IT

The complete serve is composed of many ingredients. Probably the most important is the *wrist snap*. It is an absolute must if you are to develop a powerful and effective serve.

Many players wear their arm out attempting to achieve racquet-head speed without making use of their wrist. Shoulder and elbow problems frequently arise when the player slugs the ball with an extended or stiff elbow and wrist.

A good test to determine whether you have the correct wrist-snapping technique mastered is to practice your serve with your grip in the middle of the racquet.

Start the motion with the racquet on your shoulder. Toss the ball directly over your head and flop your wrist up and over the ball. Don't muscle it. Hit up and hold the followthrough position.

Now compare it to the illustration.

Don't be surprised if the racquet handle hits you in the forearm a few times. Continue practicing until your wrist breaks properly and the handle rotates to the outside of your forearm.

Practice this drill 50 times per day until the wrist break is a natural part of your serve.

TEACH YOURSELF BY ANALYZING THE FOLLOW THROUGH

The longer the ball stays on the strings the more control you have over it.

This common axiom in tennis should be of great concern to you. No matter how good or struggling a player you are, this is what everyone strives for — better control.

To help keep the ball on the strings longer, take a look at your followthrough. The position where the racquet comes to a resting stop gives you an indication what took place during the stroke.

Next time on the court try this popular teaching drill: Hold your finish until the ball bounces on the other side of the net. Take note of its exact position.

On the forehand make these checkpoints:

1.) Check the level of your hand. If you

finish high, at the level of your eyes, this generally indicates you are attempting to lift the ball high over the net. Good.

2.) Note the position of the racquet. If it is pointed straight up and down — perpendicular — this indicates you did not make excessive use of your wrist. Good.

3.) Check the position of your arm, relative to your eyes. You should be looking over your elbow to follow the ball's flight. This generally indicates your racquet stayed with the ball for a reasonable distance. Good. (Tennis is a linear-motion skill — you hit forward and through the ball.)

4.) Finally, check your balance. If you can hold your finish until the ball bounces on the other side of the net, without moving, you pass the test. Good. Make sure your front knee is bent and your back heel is off the ground.

On the backhand the followthrough position will change depending on the type of shot you hit — topspin, flat or underspin. A general reminder, however, is to stay sideways throughout all backhands. When you finish, see if your shoulders are still perpendicular to the net. Also, your followthrough position for all three shots is high, at the level of your eyes, or higher.

Look at your serve and volleys too. Check your balance when finishing the serve. On the volleys see if you're keeping the racquet head up and catching the ball in front of your body. Check your knee bend and forward step. Give yourself a lesson.

Hit The Ball In Front

The secret to successful novice tennis is the same for championship power tennis: Hit the ball in front.

This first fundamental of stroke production, while not guaranteeing a winner on every shot, insures authoritative volleys, makes the forehand an enjoyable shot to hit, and helps prevent tennis-elbow on the backhand.

To move your point of contact forward a few inches, or a few feet, check your backswing; it's here where things go awry, making you late for the ball.

On the forehand the common problem is exaggerating the backswing; the racquet is either taken too high or too far back. As a result, timing becomes difficult on all shots coming faster than slow-motion.

To correct the over-sized forehand backswing, hold onto the racquet longer with your free hand. As you pivot your shoulders, keep your hand on the throat of the racquet until the ball bounces in front of you. Hold the racquet down below the level of your shoulders. Practice this drill a few hundred times and your abbreviated backswing will allow you to catch the ball in front.

On the backhand everybody shares the problem of preparing too late. The racquet doesn't go back until the ball bounces in front of the player; by then it's too late. The corrective suggestion is to get your shoulders turned sideways, and the racquet pulled back, before the ball reaches the net. By preparing early you'll notice a dramatic improvement in your backhand.

The key to an aggressive volley is catching the ball in front, racquet head high, with a firm grip. To check your volley technique, hold your followthrough position and see what you're doing. You should be able to tell whether you made contact in front, along side, or behind your body.

To practice these corrective changes, spend some time playing *shortcourt*. This is a practice drill played inside the service lines. The objective is to slow down your strokes, and the ball, so you can actually see the ball and racquet meet. This way you can help yourself move your point of contact further in front.

How to Play the High-Bouncing Ball

A high-bouncing ball gives most people fits.

They don't know whether to hit it up or down, catch it on the rise or when it drops, hit it flat or chip it. Usually they miss it.

So, let's learn how to hit 'em and how to return 'em.

To hit 'em:

Use your forehand; topspin the ball, if you can.

Don't try to hit a net-skimmer; wait until you get a reasonably slow, medium-bouncing ball.

Move behind the bounce; start below the ball with the racquet; lift it over the net, high and deep.

Properly executed, this shot works wonders, especially when directed to the backhand (ask Borg and Vilas). Make sure, though, you don't stand around afterwards with a big grin on your face — he may return it.

Quickly move forward, a step inside the baseline, anticipating the weak return.

To return 'em:

Move back a few steps, allowing the ball to descend to the proper hitting zone.

Try to keep the ball on your forehand side (without side-stepping into the doubles alley).

If the ball catches you by surprize, or is hit with a tremendous amount of topspin, move forward and catch it on the rise.

Lift your hand to the level of the ball; take a short backswing; bevel back the face of the racquet; drop your front shoulder; hit down and through the ball.

Aim high over the net, and deep.

Keep chipping it back until you get an opportunity to loop a forehand to his backhand.

Then move forward a step inside the baseline, and look for the weak return. . . .

TEACH YOURSELF THE LOB

One of the greatest joys in life is to send up a successful lob.

If you haven't experienced the thrill of watching some startled guy scramble back to the baseline, desperately lunge for the ball, only to rebound off the fence, it's about time you learned how to lob.

There are two types of lobs — one offensive, the other defensive — each requiring a different stroke.

The offensive lob is used to occasionally surprise the aggressive net player who likes to crowd the net. It is hit low enough so he can't run back to get it, and high enough so he can't reach it.

The technique for the offensive lob is only slightly different from that of the corresponding groundstroke. At the point of contact the racquet is beveled back a bit more. Basically, it's just a high looping forehand or backhand.

Defensive lobs are used not to surprise people, but simply to make them retreat to the baseline.

The technique entails taking a lower backswing and lifting the ball straight up in the air. It can be hit flat or with a slight amount of underspin, but it *must* be hit high.

It might help to bend your knees more so you can get underneath the ball. Use the same grip and follow through higher than usual.

Don't be timid with your lob. Hit it. Send it high enough so you have time to towel off and get back in the point.

A commonly shared problem relative to lobbing is how to return a lob. Many swing their racquet on a horizontal plane when the ball is descending on a vertical plane. The ball usually goes into the net.

To prevent this from happening, return a lob with another lob. This way you keep your stroke in the same plane as that of the ball. (Got it?)

After improving your lob, try hard to resist the urge to giggle everytime you've hit a good one. It's not polite.

Teach Yourself to RELAX

Don't you just hate those super-high lobs. They look so easy hanging up there in the air. They are easy — they're easy to miss.

The problem is having too much time to think about all the ways to flub. By the time the ball drops your muscles have tied themselves into a thousand knots.

Joe DiMaggio once described the characteristics of a good competitor: "mental concentration and physical relaxation."

He meant that it's not difficult to accomplish one or the other but it takes something extra to excel in both at the same time.

Aspiring tennis players often attempt to improve their concentration by wrinkling their brow, rounding their shoulders, stooping from the waist, squeezing their grip, and finally, pointing their racket at the opponent as if to say, "Watch out, chump!"

This ferocious warlike stance might scare someone on the football field but on the tennis court it's a waste of energy.

It would be more helpful to concentrate on relaxing. Your muscles will be in a more responsive state, giving you a better chance to get from one spot on the court to another.

Stand tall — back straight, chin up. Spread your feet comfortably and release your death-grip on the racket. Once the ball is in play, monitor your body both during and after the hit. Forget the point and the person on the other side of the net. For the moment, pay attention to you.

Notice how you move between hits. If the anxiety of anticipating the return is tying up your muscles, consciously untie them. Stay loose. Keep your heels off the court as you slide gracefully back into position.

During the stroke, check to see if you are hitting at, or through, the ball. Is there a natural completion to your stroke? If not, add one. Even if it's mechanical, affected and after the fact, bring your racket hand up to the level of your eyes following the hit.

Swing slowly and eventually you'll get the feeling of carrying the ball on the racket strings.

Spend the next couple of afternoons concentrating on relaxing. Forget the stupid score. Move lightly, keep the proper tennis posture, unclench your grip, swing slowly through the ball. And thank Joe.

Don't Get Caught In Jaws

Years ago it was known as *no-man's land* — the court area between the service and baselines you're not supposed to be caught in. Then the name was changed by a young feminist, to *no person's land*. Now the evolution of names continues — to *Jaws*.

Whatever you call it, make sure you don't spend too much time hanging around there. The danger looms that a ball may take you by surprise and hit your foot. Even if it misses, you'll find it difficult to play the ball soon after it bounces.

Always recover your court position after hitting the ball. If you have to make the play from inside the baseline, don't be caught standing around admiring your shot — get back.

One of the reasons beginning players are forgetful about moving backwards is because they're not used to moving backwards. It's unnatural. So you must occasionally practice the footwork. See how quickly you can move in reverse. Get the feet back-pedaling out of *Jaws*.

Even though the common mistake is not moving backwards, there are many situations in a match when you need to move into *Jaws*. For example, when returning a weak serve it is advisable to move into the court to play the ball at a comfortable height. Also, every player should learn to sense when his opponent is in trouble, off balance, and likely to make a weak return. When forced to play a high-bouncing ball, or a wide running shot, the player will often hit short. You can't afford to sit back watching him try for it.

After hitting a good offensive shot, putting your opponent off balance, move forward a step inside the baseline. Anticipate the short ball. At other times, if you feel he's going to rip one, move back an extra step. Learn to anticipate.

How To Win Matches by Hustling

The eventual winner of a tennis match is the player who is most determined to win. In this individual sport, when athletic skills are equal, it's not so much a battle of forehands, backhands and serves but a confrontation of wills, egotism and confidence. The weaker player concedes when convinced his opponent wants victory more than he does.

This explains why the greatest scramblers are at the top of the ladder. Evert, Connors, Borg, Solomon, Dibbs — these are tenacious players who make a superhuman effort on every ball. Their astonished opponents, instead of anticipating the return, often stand flat-footed, watching them dive and make the all-but-impossible play.

Sometimes it appears futile to extend yourself for a ball appearing to be out of reach, especially when your opponent is drooling at the net. "Why give him a chance to humiliate me? . . . If I get it back he'll only smash it away."

Nonsense. Give him a chance for an easy set up. He might get anxious and blow it.

Many players regularly give up on the shot that gets slightly behind them. When this happens to you on the backhand side, change your grip to the forehand and flick your wrist back. On the forehand side, change to a backhand grip and flip the ball up in the air. To make these shots it is necessary to relax your wrist.

If you err by hitting a dangerously short approach shot, and find yourself fearing for your safety at the net, do anything but stand there like a statue. Your opponent will either hit the ball down-the-line or cross-court. Pick one and go there; if you get lucky he'll hit it right at you. (From here you're on your own. . . .)

Another playing situation where your future appears dim is when chasing back after a successful lob. The secrets to making this difficult shot are: 1. Running past the bounce of the ball; 2. Keeping your eyes on the ball throughout the chase; and 3. Staying to one side of the ball, preferably the forehand. If you let the ball drop low you'll have a better chance to make a high defensive lob.

Play up to your potential in tennis. Be enthusiastic on the court and you'll show your opponent you want to win more than he does — and you will.

DON'T ADMIRE
YOUR SHOTS

THE "UNRETURNABLE" SHOT

You've just hit a beautiful forehand down the line. What a shot! The ball sails into the corner as you watch your astonished opponent take off in pursuit. . . .

"Run, turkey!" you cry, as he scrambles for the ball. "He'll never get it without breaking his neck." You smile as he desperately lunges for the ball. . . .

"O (expletive deleted)!" you shout. "He got it!" You take off for his weak cross court backhand and get it — on the third bounce.

You've learned your lesson: Don't stand there admiring your shots!

Even though you're surprised and happy, you must resist the urge. As soon as you play the ball, prepare for the return.

If you are exchanging hits from the baseline, make sure you move to anticipate the cross-court return as soon as you've played the ball.

When at the net, follow the flight of your shot and cover the down the line return. Your footwork is just as critical after you hit the ball as before you hit it.

TENNIS IS SIMILAR TO CHESS

Tennis is like chess. It takes the same kind of patience to be a winner.

In many sports, impulsiveness and aggression are attributes. Not so with this one. In tennis the player is rewarded if he can keep his cool, sit back, and wait for the big opportunity. The guy who can't wait to hit winners is usually punished in defeat.

Impatient players often employ the scare tactic — hit a weak shot and rush the net. They draw attention by slapping their feet on the court as they approach. Their startled opponents are so surprised they can't return the ball. It's a great strategic plan — against a lousy player. When attempted against an experienced player the net rusher often ends up wearing the ball.

Play tennis like chess. Plan your shots in a sequential pattern. Think of each point as you would a chess opening. Plan it out.

In order to play *chess tennis*, you must realize most points are lost from the baseline. Because of the limited angles from the backcourt, it's difficult to hit winners. So don't attempt ridiculous shots when you (and your opponent) are back.

At the baseline strategically plan your *opening*. Do this by playing the ball high over the net and deep. If you clear the net by six feet the ball will bounce high, forcing your opponent to move back behind the baseline to play it. This keeps his angles small and gives you a better chance to force a weak return.

As your game improves you'll develop confidence with different shots that force your opponents into weak returns and errors. You will learn how to move him by changing the angle of the ball.

You'll be able to hit it where he ain't. This will elicit a weak return and an opportunity to approach the net. It's here where you finally have a chance for a dramatic putaway.

Even though you make it to the forecourt, don't be reckless. Continue to work for an opening. If you are standing near the service line you may not have sufficient angle to hit a winner. Also, if the ball is low (below tape level), you can't be too fancy. You'll have to continue with your pattern until you find yourself with an open court and an angle. Then go for it!

Everything comes to him who waits.

How to Concentrate on the Ball Better

Learn to concentrate on the ball. Tennis teachers have almost worn out the command *"Watch the Ball!"* Yet it is still heard frequently. Actually the phrase should read: *"Concentrate on the Ball!"* This is more appropriate because most people are able to watch the ball. The problem is the physical possibility of seeing the ball, as well as your opponent, the match on the court next to you, and the good-looking girl (or guy) three courts away.

Really lock in on the ball. Squint at it as your opponent tosses the ball up for his serve, refocus your eyes when it bounces in front of you. See the ball at two different times: once when it leaves the racquet and again just before you hit it. The ball should appear larger the second time you see it, enlarging from the size of a golf ball to the size of a softball in a second.

Watch the seams of the ball. If you can, then try to see the writing on the ball. If that's possible, try to decipher what it says. (Is it a Wilson, Penn, or Dunlop.) If you can tell the difference, then probably you can also *leap tall buildings with a single bound.*

Always remind yourself that the ball loses much of its speed after it hits the ground. Don't let yourself get psyched-out by the big hitter. Learn to anticipate better, react quicker, and concentrate on the ball.

You should also concentrate on the ball between points. For example, if you've just missed a forehand and the ball is lying at the bottom of the net, slowly walk to the ball and examine it for a moment. In your mind, replay the shot you just missed, this time hitting it perfectly.

Deliberately pick up the ball and, if your opponent is serving, send the ball back to him with a forehand. If you are serving, walk slowly back to the baseline, bouncing the ball as you glare at it — all the time thinking positively.

COMPETE AGAINST YOURSELF, NOT YOUR OPPONENT

When you first get started in tennis, one of the worst things that can happen is to have an unreturnable serve.

In the evolution of your game a big serve retards the process. You don't hit enough balls.

Although some athletic beginners discover that by rushing the net they'll win a few points, against a good player they get passed or lobbed.

The more balls you hit (in the court), the better player you become.

If you accept this axiom, then your objective, in practice and in competition, should be to keep the ball in play as long as possible. Problems arise, however, when you anticipate your opponent will err and he hits a winner against you. Immediately you set out for revenge.

Eventually your match ends in a slugfest — each trying to outdo the other. Your strategic objective is to finish the point as expeditiously as possible. "Beat 'em before he beats you."

Take a tip from the pros. Improve your game by developing your skills in keeping the ball in play. Instead of competing against your opponent, compete against yourself.

You can learn this by counting your (own) hits in each point. You may be surprised to see how few times you hit three balls in a row.

Unfortunately, it's natural to judge yourself when competing during a match. Usually you judge yourself in terms of winning or losing each point, and it doesn't matter how you do it — by hitting a winner at the end of a long rally or being handed the point when your opponent double-faults. Either way, you win.

By counting your hits, the first judgment you make at the end of a point is, "How many hits did I make?" This is a positive self-judgment. Even if you lose a long rally, there's consolation in the fact you made a number of consecutive hits.

Someday, when you can average three hits per point, consider yourself a good, steady, mature tennis player.

HOW
TO MOVE
LIKE A TENNIS
PLAYER

Chris Evert is amazing to watch. She gives you the impression she isn't trying. For some reason she always seems to be where the ball is. She hardly has to run.

Her sixth sense — anticipation — is more than just playing experience and a keen eye — it's also movement. She knows how to handle her body so she can move effortlessly.

In anxious anticipation of your opponent's next move it is possible you psyche yourself into a position where you can't react. You want to move so bad your muscles rebel, leaving you half-frozen in fear.

Somehow the typical weekend player erroneously assumes he has a better chance to improve his reflexes if he puts himself in, what he thinks is, the proper ready position. By trying to get ready the player often prohibits his body from being responsive. He digs his chin into his chest, hunches over from the back, stands with his legs straight, and grips his racquet as if someone was trying to take it away from him. The player transforms himself into an immovable object. He's cement.

Don't let this happen to you. Instead of *trying* to get ready after playing the ball, try not to try — stay loose. In a backcourt rally quickly start sliding back into position once you've played the ball. Do not cross your feet as you recover. Stand tall from the waist and bend your knees. Be rhythmical. As you slide make an attempt to keep your weight on the balls of your feet. Don't let your heels touch the ground. Consciously relax your shoulders and the grip on your racquet.

The subtle secret of sure-footed anticipation is being in motion when the ball is hit. You must learn to time your footwork so you're moving (sideways) in the direction you think the ball will return. When rallying from the baseline, this usually means crosscourt. If you hit down-the-line, quickly start sliding so you'll be well on your way toward the opposite side of the court when the ball is contacted.

A good habit to develop at the net is the *bounce step*. This will help cut off those sneaky passing shots. Just as your opponent strikes the ball split your feet wide and bounce gently on your toes. With your feet spread you're less likely to step with the wrong foot when volleying.

Don't try so hard. Trust your natural reflexes. Give them a chance to work for you. Be loose and in motion as the ball is played. You'll get there before it does.

Practice Hitting the Ball in the Court

Tennis is easier to learn if you practice hitting the ball in the court.

That's opposed to hitting it in the net, wide of the court, against and over the fence.

Your objective is learning to control the ball. With this clearly in mind your game improves almost daily. Right away you discover an ability to not only hit the ball in the court, but someplace in the court.

In serving, instead of just trying to get it in "that little square," you'll find it possible to aim it.

No kidding. You'll actually be able to hit it where you want it to go — like to your opponent's backhand.

In your baseline rallies you'll be able to hit it crosscourt or down-the-line, high over the net and deep, or low over the net and short.

Your newfound versatility will make tennis an entirely different experience. It'll be more fun than you ever imagined.

All you have to do is start trying to direct it. You might have to slow down a little. Obviously, if you're still missing, slow down some more.

From now on, in practice and in matches, try to hit every ball in the court, someplace.

THE FEATHER SHOTS IN TENNIS

There's nothing more devastating in tennis than the drop-shot-and-lob combination. It's like playing with a yo-yo. First you draw him into the net with a delicately placed drop-shot, then, when he gets there, you float one over his head. Properly executed, it's one of tennis' great satisfactions. Unfortunately, it's a pleasure relatively few players ever experience. Most do not relax enough to hit soft shots. They hit everything with a clenched fist, at one speed — fast.

Touch shots are fun. They are another of the game's elements, making tennis what it is (or should be).

The most apparent touch shot is the drop-shot. It is played from well inside the baseline, initiating as a regular groundstroke. At the last moment the racquet bevels underneath the ball, creating underspin and a bounce that *dies*.

The keys to the drop-shot are disguise and underspin. Underspin dictates the type of bounce the ball will have — the lower the better. To produce this effect, hit up and through the ball with the racquet face tilted back. Relax your grip and arm; let the racquet almost fall out of your hand. The trajectory of the ball's flight should be up, not down. Clear the net by at least one foot. Let underspin do the dirty work.

Learning touch shots is critical in developing an all-around game. Even though you shouldn't try the tricky drop shot too often, it is important you have the potential to finesse the ball. After all, your soft shots are what make your power shots more effective. For example, your passing shot wouldn't be too successful if you couldn't surprise your opponent with an occasional lob. And your biggest serve will be for naught if you can't scoop up a low half-volley.

So, instead of always trying to power the passing shot down-the-line, try hitting an angled underspin crosscourt. Learn to shift gears. The change in speed produces a change in rhythm, which will likely produce a confused opponent.

Spend the next couple of weeks practicing your feather shots. Bring your opponents into the net, then practice your lob. In your rallies hit every other shot as soft as possible. Discover the fun of controlling the speed and rhythm of the game. After you develop the feel of the touch shots, consider yourself a more complete tennis player.

HOW TO PRACTICE THE SERVICE TOSS

Are you having trouble tossing the ball on your serve? If so, it's probably due to the fact that you're tossing the ball.

The service toss is really not a toss at all — it's more of a placement. The tennis ball only weighs two ounces. Properly executed, it does not require much energy to place it in the correct spot. Here's how to practice:

Stand in front of a pole or in the corner of a room. Your left foot should point at a 45 degree angle to the vertical line. Hold the ball between your thumb and fingers. Extend your arm so that it is perfectly straight. Lower your arm so the back of your hand is resting against the inside of your left thigh. From here lift your stiffened arm up in a line with your left foot. Release the ball at the highest point possible. Don't throw it! Pretend you are setting the ball on a shelf. Open your fingers and thumb simultaneously so the ball will not spin. Leave your hand extended and the ball should fall back into it. Practice without the racquet 25 times. Don't forget to catch the ball with your arm extended; that's important.

Now take the racquet and try synchronizing your arms. . . . Down together — touch your thigh — up together. . . . Catch and hold. . . . Practice 25 times and then take the acid test.

Close your eyes and see if the ball falls back into your hand. (Don't forget to close your mouth!)

AIM HIGHER TO HIT
THE BALL DEEPER

This is another in a never-ending series of chapters on hitting the ball deep in the court.

Although you may have good intentions, for some reason your serve usually falls short, your groundstrokes often land inside the service line, and your lobs are always smashed away for winners.

It's probably not your technique that's to blame for these strategic errors (you could possess perfect textbook strokes and still hit the ball short) — the reason you underhit your shots is simply that you aim too low.

These mental miscalculations are often made because the player aims at the service line for the serve, and the baseline for the groundstrokes. Standing at the opposite end of the court, his perspective is deceiving: he looks down at the target. So he hits down.

And gravity makes the ball land short.

The goal in this game is to make your opponent regularly play the ball from a position behind the baseline. From there he won't have sufficient angle to do you harm. If he tries, you'll be pleased to see his shots fall into the net or go wide.

To accomplish that goal, aim at an imaginary spot above the net. If you want your groundstrokes to land within four feet of the baseline, aim six feet over the net and note where they go.

You may need to increase your net clearance to increase your depth; in fact, it's necessary for many players to aim a couple feet higher than their intended target, to reach it.

Throughout the entire match take note of your results. The tendency is to hit short when the situation gets tense or the player begins to tire. When either of these things begins to happen, consciously aim higher over the net.

Again, strategy in tennis is basically very simple: keep the ball deep so your opponent will hit short so you'll have some angle to work with.

Aim high.

HOW TO GET MORE CENTER HITS

When a player hits more balls off the wood than the strings, he begins to wonder if there's something wrong with his eyesight.

100

He's more than embarrassed when some smart-aleck shouts, "Use the strings — your racquet will last longer!"

Better players have problems too. The intermediate often overhits the ball, trying to compensate for mishitting and to gain pace. The advanced player realizes that a mishit volley will often turn an attempted winner into an easy passing shot. Hitting in the center of the racquet is no easy task. It takes years before one can expect to hit just one out of three balls in the *sweet spot*.

The ability to hit the ball squarely and with authority is what determines the eventual winner. Here's how you can improve this ability:

— **Don't be violent.** Overhitting is a circular pattern that leads nowhere. The immature player mishits a ball, so he swings harder the following shot. Again he mishits it, which prompts him to swing even harder. It's like the baseball player wildly whiffing the air, trying for a home run, or a crazy weekend golfer straining to drive the ball like Jack Nicklaus. Center hits in all sports are only achieved by controlling the body with a conservative backswing and economical motion.

— **Keep your balance.** Mishits frequently occur if the player is not set at the point of contact. Be on balance. Step prior to the hit and keep your front foot flat during the hit. Bend your knees. To test your balance, try holding your finish for two counts after each hit. *Be a statue.*

— **See the ball.** Many players can't wait to see where their shot is going, so they look before hitting it. This causes lots of disappointing mishits. Keep your head steady, eyes fixed to the point of contact until the ball is gone. Watch the ball carefully. Focus on it twice: once as it is being hit, and then as you contact it. Notice how it enlarges the second time. Can you see the seams of the ball?

The following drills will help exercise your skills at making center contact. Hold the racquet in the middle with only three fingers (choke up). Turn the racquet face up and dribble the ball up. Don't send it higher than 12 inches.

Try bouncing it down repetitively holding the racquet with the same grip. You will become very sensitive about making deadcenter contact. If you mishit the ball, the racquet will turn in your hand.

Practice against a backboard with the same grip. On the court, try rallying from the baseline with a loose grip. The extra concentration will help.

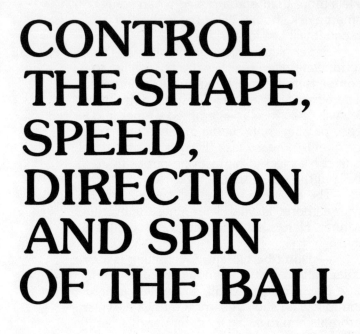

CONTROL THE SHAPE, SPEED, DIRECTION AND SPIN OF THE BALL

"He's a magician. He can do anything with the ball."

This is the best compliment a tennis player can receive. It means the player is so masterful at controlling the tennis ball, he can influence its shape, speed, direction and spin.

From the novice player's first introduction to tennis, he should be encouraged to control the ball, even though the temptation to smash, kill, beat, slug and thrash around is almost irresistible.

You must treat the tennis ball with respect, and become friends with it, to eventually have it respond to your commands.

The first step is to (begin to) learn how to control the shape, or flight of the ball. As you rally from the baseline, experiment by sending the ball various heights over the net. Alternate your shots in a pattern: hit the first ball just barely over the net; hit the second one approximately five feet over; and the third about ten feet over. The goal is to learn how to vary the shape of your shot depending on the playing situation: low shots to drop at the net rusher's feet, medium-high shots for deep baseline rallies, and high shots for lobbing over the net player.

Learning to control the direction of the ball is a never-ending process. At the beginning stages most shots are defensively played down the middle of the court — as far from a line as possible. Later, the player tries to occasionally direct the ball to his opponent's backhand. Eventually he can hit down-the-line or cross-court. Several years later he can change the angle of the ball, hitting it where the other guy isn't. All along the way, the player hits very few balls wide; he always gives himself a comfortable margin for error.

Controlling the speed of the ball is something the beginning/intermediate should learn as he first tries to control its shape and trajectory. Again, his objective is to eventually be able to set the tempo of the rallies and change the speed of his shots at will.

Finally, after a couple of years of working on the above, the player learns how to make the ball work for him by controlling its spin. This way his shots produce an effect — topspin travels faster and bounces higher, underspin travels slower and bounces lower.

Be a magician — (begin to) learn how to control the ball.

103

VOLLEY OUT NOT DOWN

How many disappointing times have you taken an easy volley putaway and put it right in the bottom of the net?

Hurts, doesn't it?

The reason so many of these setups are so tragically missed has to do with the angle of the racquet face at impact. Instead of being tilted back, the racquet meets the ball in a "closed," or turned down position.

This technical error repeatedly occurs because the player fails to make the necessary change in racquet angle upon reaching the net.

At the baseline, flat and top-spin shots are hit with the racquet face perpendicular to the ground, but at the net the racquet must be beveled back to successfully play the low volley and also to keep the ball deep. Contrary to how it appears, the volley is hit out, not down.

Since most players learn the ground strokes before the volleys, it is understandable why they make a few errors up there. At the baseline they develop the technique of taking a backswing and following through; at the net this "stroke" causes trouble.

The volley is hardly a stroke at all; in fact, it might help for you to consider it nothing more than a blocking motion. All you do is reach forward and intercept the ball in front. Push the bottom edge of the racquet forward, hold on tight, and send the ball deep. (Even when you're standing on top of the net, volley out.)

A helpful corrective drill is to glance at your racquet immediately after contacting the ball. At first you'll have a tendency to follow the ball with your eyes; ignore it as it leaves your racquet. Look at the spot where you made contact. The racquet head should be above your wrist and tilted back. Your goal is to hit it far enough in front so you can see the back of the racquet frame.

A few 10-minute practice sessions will prevent countless disheartening experiences at the net.

How to Smooth Out Your Strokes

Give your game a diagnostic check. If your serve "backfires," your backhand "misses," and your forehand "sputters," your game needs a minor tune-up.

Your tennis is analogous to a smooth-running engine. Timing, rhythm and effortless motion make it work. The same attributes make for a consistent and effective game of tennis. It may take years to completely iron out those wrinkled strokes and be a smooth hitter, but there are things you can do today that will immediately help you play with more poise and finesse.

The first suggestion is to tame your strokes down. It's difficult to feel your muscles if your body is out of control. Try hitting some balls in slow motion. See how slow you can go. Forget the ball for a moment — concentrate on your muscles.

As you rally in slow motion, draw your

attention to the exact moment you begin to take the racquet back. Where is the ball when you begin to prepare? Is it at the net? . . . bouncing? . . . on top of you? It's difficult to be a fluid player if you do not prepare early. To help this problem, see if you can begin your backswing as your opponent ends his follow-through. Make it an exercise in rhythm.

A final suggestion is to talk yourself into being smooth. As you swing your racquet through the ball, say "smoooth." Mesmerize yourself by following your verbal directions. Say it slowly while you concentrate on the timing of the hit and the word clue.

The longer the ball lingers on the strings, the more control you'll have over its direction. So slow down - prepare as soon as possible - and talk yourself through it. Practice diligently and someday you'll be a graceful, fluid, smooth-running, tennis motor-machine.

Lob More, Lob Higher

"The lob is the measure of a player's worth."

Chances are whoever first said that was either an excellent judge of tennis talent, or had a heck of a good lob.

Today the top male and female players are both possessors of deadly accurate lobs.

Analyzing the tactics of Jimmy Connors reveals that, at the beginning of a match, his first few defenses against the net player are often lobs. Later in the match the crowd marvels at his penetrating passing shots, but it was his lob that made those screamers possible.

Respecting his lob, Jimmy's opponents stop near the service line, giving him better angles with which to pass.

You too can teach your opponents to respect your lob, by practicing it more often.

Next time on the court give your lob a test. Purposely hit a short ball, draw your opponent into net, and throw up a lob.

Beware of the common lobbing mistake: aiming too low. Although this tactic produces an occasional offensive winner, the even greater number of successful smashes should tell you something.

Lob higher. Hit it almost as high as you can.

After you discover the proper height of your lobs, keep practicing until you can regularly lob high and deep.

Then tell your friends how a player's worth is measured.

You Can't Serve Down into the Court

Watching the average club-level player on the court is puzzling. It's difficult to understand why he repeatedly dumps his first serve into the bottom of the net and resorts to pushing his second one to get the point started.

The common misconception here is that the player thinks he can hit the serve down into the court — a la Pancho Gonzales' flat *cannonball* serve. Forget it! Unless you are 6 ft. 7 in. and have a reach of ten feet, you will not have the necessary height to serve directly down into the court.

You must hit up and forward to develop a consistent and forceful serve — not down. Here's how you can improve your serving effectiveness immediately:

Check your service toss. Although John Newcombe tosses the ball four feet into the court and makes contact with his feet nine inches off the ground, you must realize that you're not John Newcombe. Serve on balance.

Try tossing the ball so that it falls back on your forehead. You can only hit from up here.

Practice a "sit-down" serve. Take a basket of balls and practice your serve from a sitting position (on your right knee). Start at the service line. Choke-up on the racquet and start the motion with your racquet resting on your right shoulder. Toss the ball over your head and flop your wrist over it so the handle ends up outside your forearm. Serve the next basket from a point half way between the service line and baseline — and the next basket from the baseline.

Now stand up and try the whole motion. Let ball rotation (topspin) and gravity work for you. If you've done everything properly you've lost 50 per cent of your power but gained 500 per cent more control. Keep practicing until you can direct it and someday you'll own a serve that will be an asset instead of a liability.

111

HOW TO WATCH THE BALL BETTER

One of the most common mistakes made by tennis players is to prematurely look to see where the ball is going before it is actually hit. This problem is also shared by golfers and baseball players — and in all other sports which involve hitting an object with an implement.

The popular time-worn suggestion for people who suffer this malady is to *watch the ball*. Some teachers plead with their students to see the ball and racquet meet on every hit.

Whether this is physically possible is a matter of discussion. The real crux is that the player's head is motionless at the point of contact. This ensures a better chance to make a center hit — an occurrence that many players rarely experience.

A more practical suggestion for you is to watch the spot where the ball used to be. This is a trick that many tournament players use to keep their head and eyes on the approaching

ball. Keep your head steady at the point of contact, looking at the spot where you made contact.

Try this technique first in practice. Serve the ball, keeping your chin and eyes up until the ball is gone. It will feel strange at first. You'll think you're missing something. Say to yourself, "see blue" — as you serve. Look up toward the sky and you'll actually see the racquet hitting up and through the ball.

Hit your groundstrokes the same way. Watch the spot. Say "see green" — just after making contact with the ball.

Get in the good habit of hitting all your shots with your eyes hesitating on the spot where the ball used to be. If it helps Billie Jean King, it'll help you.

Underspin:
When and Why to Use It

In most playing situations in tennis there are two basic strategies: offense and defense. As in football and baseball, the players must know their responsibilities in each situation.

Many players pick a style of play that fits their personality. This explains why the courts are filled with free-swinging aggressive players. If you consider yourself a take-it-to-em player — and you're interested in becoming a complete player — learn how to play defensive tennis as well.

A defensive shot is the answer to an offensive shot. There are many times in this game when you need a defensive play to keep yourself in the point. Since more offensive shots are hit with topspin, defensive shots are generally hit with underspin.

The first situation that calls for a defensive underspin shot is the service return. When faced with a high-hopping serve, simply abbreviate your backswing, bevel the face of the racquet and swing through the ball. Neutralize the pace of the ball by sending it back with underspin.

When returning any forceful shot it is wise to utilize underspin. If you are being chased unmercifully around the court, slow up the pace of the ball with a high underspin crosscourt floater. This will give you time to catch your breath, recover lost position, and get back in the point.

At the top levels of play underspin is used to change the shape and bounce of the ball. Good players constantly vary their shots to keep their opponents off balance. Baseline players like to hit short underspin balls to their opponent's backhand. If he comes in, they'll try to pass him; if he moves back, they'll try to follow it up with a deep crosscourt to his forehand.

Approach the net with underspin. You need time to get there, and the low bounce will often make your opponent pop the ball up to you.

Place your volleys deep in the court with underspin. Bevel the racquet and block through the ball. Finish the shot with the bottom edge of the racquet forward.

Most backhands are hit with underspin. Anatomically, it's a much easier shot to hit and control. Slide through the ball and finish high.

Learn the tactics that make the good guys good. Use underspin.

BEND YOUR KNEES, PLEASE

"Watch the ball, bend your knees — that'll be 20 dollars, please."

Tennis instruction is often so basic that it's boring. The rudiments of the game, while easy to learn, are like any other valued skill. They are difficult to master.

Their worth becomes apparent in a match between two players who are otherwise equal. The one that makes fewer fundamental mistakes will win. And winning seldom is boring.

One of the most valuable lessons to be learned is the simplest — bend the knees when hitting the ball. Sounds easy, but many students have to put considerable physical and mental effort into it before the habit develops.

It's much easier to be lazy and play the ball from the waist, keeping the legs straight. The mistakes caused by this carelessness are many.

First of all, it's tough to play the ball well

when it drops below the *hitting zone*. By standing straight up and dropping the racquet head, the player loses his *feel*. His hand-eye coordination is much better when the racquet head is up, where it should be. To achieve that, he must lower his body by bending his knees.

Secondly, a bent knee at the point of contact usually indicates the player has moved his weight forward into the stroke. This, above all else, contributes to effortless, yet forceful shots.

Lastly, bending the knee insures a balanced hit. The knee functions as a shock absorber. If the player hurriedly approaches the ball stiff-legged, he's likely to lose his balance and flub the shot. Bending the knee absorbs the shock of foot against court and smooths the approach, ensuring better rhythm.

Rhythm is vital. The cadence should be: *Step and hit*. If the front knee bends with the step, the racquet head will come through cleanly and smoothly. There isn't much margin for error. Any sudden, jerky motion will result in an off-center hit, and probably a mistake.

Knees, knees, knees. Bend them on your groundstrokes, bend them on your lob. Scrape them on the court when stretching for a low volley. On every shot in practice, tell yourself: "Bend." A good habit will follow.

Now, getting back to the 20 dollars. . . .

BE AGGRESSIVE AT NET

Strategy and tactics change dramatically once you reach the net. Back at the baseline your goal was to make as few unforced errors as possible; however, at the net your personality must change. From a timid, restraining baseline player, you must transform into an aggressive opportunist.

Developing the killer instinct for many players is difficult; some just hate to end things. They'll play a long point from the baseline, work their way into the net, set up an easy volley winner — and obligingly hit it right back to their waiting opponent. Walking back to baseline they wonder to themselves, "Why in the _____ didn't I put it away?"

It's frustrating. One moment you need the patience of a surgeon — the next you could use the rashness of an alley fighter. It's a special combination of skills that make a tennis champion.

Time is crucial at the net. In less than a split second you must react to put the ball away. Top level players develop instinctive reflexes that cover every situation. So can you.

One of the essentials of good net play is aggressive footwork. Moving forward to intercept the ball, rather than allowing it to come to you, may be the missing ingredient in your game.

First of all, position yourself so you can move quickly to either side. Spread your feet wide so your head is almost at the level of the net tape. Keep your back straight and hold your racquet directly in front of your body.

Again, the objective is to move forward. To exaggerate the idea, step in a line toward the net posts. (On the forehand volley the right-handed player steps toward the right net post with his left foot.) This is called the CROSS-OVER STEP. It will turn your shoulders perpendicular to the net and help you meet the ball in front. (On the backhand volley your right foot crosses in front of your left to make the play; step towards the left net post.)

The cross-over step should take place before the ball is contacted. During your next practice session make the step as quick as possible. To judge your quickness, slap your foot on the court prior to the hit. *Slap and hit. . . . slap and hit.* Hear the cadence.

Show some razzle-dazzle out there. Get prepared — move forward with the cross-over step — meet the ball in front — and finish the point!

How to Practice Against the Backboard

If you're a beginner and you're having problems finding someone to play tennis with, then introduce yourself to the local backboard.

There's probably one at the nearest junior or senior high school or recreation center.

Before you make a bad impression on your new "partner," read and follow these step-by-step directions:

1.) Hit the ball ever-so-softly. If you swing too hard, the ball will come back faster than you'll be able to prepare for the next stroke.

2.) When you practice your groundstrokes, aim high against the board so the ball will provide you with a nice bounce, which will also give you time to get ready.

3.) Follow through. Make sure you complete your stroke. By slowing down and aiming high, you should have time to momentarily hold your finish before returning to a ready position.

4.) If you absolutely insist on belting the ball, move back, allowing it to bounce twice before striking it again. Although this is generally not a good habit to develop, it's probably better than frustrating yourself by trying to keep a rally going.

5.) Occasionally check your point-of-contact positions. Stand about ten feet away from the board and gently tap the ball without taking a backswing. Focus your eyes on the racquet frame after the ball leaves the strings. (Your objective is to contact the ball in front of your front hip, on balance, foot flat, knee bent, leaning forward.)

6.) When you've slowed yourself down and can usually meet the ball in front, practice alternating groundstrokes — forehand, backhand, forehand, backhand, etc. You'll have to move quickly between the strokes so you can address the ball properly.

7.) Whenever you feel yourself begin to lose control of the ball, on any drill, stop the ball and start the rally again. You want to prevent the frantic, out-of-control flailing that many people exhibit against the backboard.

8.) Lastly, once in a while look around and see if there's another lonely soul whose only partner is the backboard. When you find someone, stop your rally, walk over, get their attention, boldly step forward, introduce yourself and say, "Wanna hit some?"

Detecting and Correcting the "Pancake Serve"

Maybe you have one. It's called the *pancake serve* — a.k.a. the *shot put, flyswatter, marshmallow* or *push* serve. All are different names for the type of serves that many tennis players rely on — the push-it-in-and-play serve. The objective of this serve is only to get the point started — nothing else.

Many players adopt this style of serving because of their anatomical inability to throw properly. They do it because their muscles don't respond any other way. In order to learn the motion that makes it possible to develop an aggressive serve, they must learn to throw. This can be accomplished partly by familiarizing themselves with the following three checkpoints:

(1) **Use the correct grip.** You're doomed to a lifetime of lousy serving if you don't change your grip. You probably now use a *Western forehand* grip. Move the palm of your hand so it is over the top right bevel of the handle. This will make it possible for you to learn *slice* and *spin* serves.

(2) **Check your** *poised-for power* **position.** It's here where things might break down. Toss the ball up, swing the racquet back and hold that position as you catch the ball. Don't move. Check the position of your right elbow. It should be at the level of your shoulder. Now look over your left shoulder and check the position of the racquet head. If you can't see anything, position it behind your left ear. Make

sure the strings are on edge — parallel to your back.

(3) **The wrist snap.** Hit a couple of balls, holding the racquet in the middle of the handle. Try to stop the followthrough just after the point of contact. Check two things: (1) the height at which you contacted the ball (reach up) and, (2) the evidence of a wrist break. (The handle should have rotated to the outside of your forearm.)

If you promise yourself to enthusiastically practice these three checkpoints you will make it possible to one day change from a *pancake* serve to a *dyn-o-mite* serve.

123

What, Why, When and How to
Practice

Is your game on a holding pattern? Was the last time you noticed significant improvement when you learned the correct grips? Many struggling intermediate players fight their tennis for years, never improving their level of play. If you would like to get serious about your game, get serious about practicing.

Practice means uninterrupted sessions of repetitive hitting. It's the surest way to move up the ladder.

Pick your weakest area. Forget everything else for a few weeks and promise yourself to improve this one weakness. First you must discover why you are having problems. This will entail taking a tennis lesson, watching a good player and making a comparison, or maybe reading a book. Whatever you do, don't make the mistake of practicing without knowing exactly what and how to practice.

Find an obliging partner with an interest in working on his game. You should have some practice balls and a court where you won't interrupt play around you.

Warm up slowly. Start your workout by standing near the service lines and gradually move back. Control your muscles in slow-motion. Feel the correct technique. Later, as you reach the baseline, slowly open the throttle. Hit the ball with as much pace as possible — still controlling it.

Use targets in your practice. Set tennis cans on the court and learn to direct the ball. If your strokes are good, but you have problems hitting where you want, set up a target and practice a new shot. Remember, you should never try a shot in a match that you haven't mastered first in practice.

One hour of constant drilling is plenty. Always quit your practice on a positive note. Stop only after a good series of hits. This will help keep you psyched up for the next session.

The difference between a champ and a loser is often just a few key points. And sometimes you lose these points because a weakness is exposed and you get a bit nervous. To protect this from happening, practice your weak shots. Usually these shots are the ones you hit the least. If you never hit enough volleys and overheads, play a game of *half-speed tennis*. This game can be played where you play the entire point at half-speed — or you can play only the first two hits at half-speed — then anything goes.

How often should you practice? That depends on how much you play. A general rule is to have one practice session for *every* three times you play.

To keep your game continually growing, always remember this popular educational proverb: *perfect practice makes perfect*.

HOW TO APPROACH THE NET

A warning sign should be posted on every court; its message: CAUTION — APPROACH NET AT YOUR OWN RISK.

Many preventable accidents occur because of the careless net rusher. The sorriest victim is the guy who momentarily loses his head, lobs, and rushes the net. Such tactical errors can be dangerous to one's physical well being. A prudent suggestion is to read the following ten safety precautions regarding approach shots.

1.) Before deciding to follow your serve into net, make sure it is strong enough so you'll feel secure as you run in behind it.

2.) Avoid serving to the forehand and coming in, especially on the deuce court where the right hander has a good angle to pass you; if you must, try it on the ad court, but sparingly.

3.) Be selective when approaching the net. Make sure you are well inside the baseline when contacting the ball. At the beginning levels of play only come in when forced to (when it is impossible for you to retreat to the baseline). As you improve, the main consideration is that you get close enough to the net following the approach shot so you can make an effective first volley.

4.) Regard the approach shot as a means of transportation — it paves your way into the net. The objective is to place your opponent on the defensive so you'll have a good opportunity to subsequently put the ball away. It is a means to an end. Don't over-hit the ball trying for a winner.

5.) Hit the ball at the top of its bounce. Bevel the racquet face back and use underspin; it will give you more time to reach the net — plus it produces a low bounce, which forces your opponent to hit the ball up. Take a short backswing, turn sideways, and stroke through the ball.

6.) Follow the flight of the ball to the net. This will help position yourself so you can cover the opponent's widest two possible returns.

7.) Stop your forward momentum before he makes contact with the ball. Take into consideration the depth of your approach. If your approach is deep, stop short, near the service line, anticipating a lob. If you hit shallow, move forward and look for the passing shot. Stop with both feet at the same time — like a hopscotch step.

8.) Hit your approach deep, preferably to the backhand. Sacrifice pace for placement.

9.) Generally, hit your approach down-the-line. This makes it easier to get in position for the volley. Only approach crosscourt for an occasional surprise.

10.) A short ball is an invitation to the net you do not have to accept. If your opponent possesses an uncanny lob, or a penetrating passing shot, use your discretion — refuse his invitation — stay back and wait him out.

127

How to Keep From Getting Hurt at the Net

At the net it's instinctive to take a full swing at the ball.

In most cases though, there isn't enough time to wind up, make contact, and expect it to go in. From the time the baseline layer hits the ball until it reaches the net player, less than one second elapses — hardly enough time to do anything fancy.

The volley usually is a reflex action. There's little time to think, plan or prepare. It's simply an automatic reaction. To be a successful net player you have to learn the *reflex volley*.

The main difference between the reflex volley and the average hacker's volley is the first move: the hacker moves back when he should move forward.

To help prepare you for that move, it is important to get ready properly. Stand halfway between the service line and the net. Spread your feet wide. This will help you move laterally faster. Bend your knees and pretend you are riding a horse — bounce!

You should almost be sitting down while standing up. Hold your racquet at arm's length directly in front, with the left hand at the throat. Both arms are straight. The racquet head is high, at the level of your eyes. Concentrate and anticipate.

Here comes the ball! Don't let it come to you — go forward to meet it. Take a long stride forward to intercept it close to the net. Bend your knees, stepping forward with the foot farthest away from the ball.

On the forehand, simply lay your wrist back and block the ball with the bottom edge of racquet forward. Underspin produces depth, control and a low bounce. (Don't chop at it to produce this spin.)

Try to play your volleys at eye level. Bend your knees lower. Until you get stronger, change grips for the backhand and do the same.

No matter how great your volley is, don't stand there saying, "Gotcha!" It never pays. Immediately get your free hand on the throat of the racquet and recover to your ready position. Ole!

ERP
is the Key
to a Better
Overhead

The overhead smash is the average hacker's first opportunity to take out all his frustrations and kill the ball. It's usually the only opportunity in the game to hit directly down into the court. Most people blow it.

They don't *erp* soon enough. What? They simply don't get the racquet prepared to hit the ball. Maybe someone has told them that the overhead motion is like the service. So when the lob goes up they start imitating their service toss: Down together . . . up together. By the time they get the racquet on their shoulder the ball has bounced off their forehead.

Early racquet preparation (erp) is the key to success on the overhead. Don't waste time getting the racquet into the *cocked position.* Pretend you're an archer and you are reaching for an arrow in the quiver. Reach straight back over your shoulder. Now turn sideways and get your free hand up in the air to follow the flight of the ball. Actually point at the ball. Use your hand as a point of reference. Skip step behind and under the ball. Now reach up as high as you can and crunch it. Keep your chin up and don't forget to use your wrist as you crack it away for a winner. . . . You missed again? Don't worry, the overhead is usually the last shot developed in tennis. Keep practicing!

131

PICK YOUR OPPONENTS WISELY

The big search in tennis is looking for someone better to play. This seems to be every serious player's main concern — finding someone who's better, but not too much better, to play with. (You don't want to get depressed.)

As a result of this selectiveness, local tennis courts and clubs sometimes become *cliquish*. A's (the best players) don't want to play with B's (better club players), B's don't want anything to do with C's (average club players), C's can't stand D players (advanced beginners), and D's thumb their noses at F players (beginners — who are humble and happy).

Playing up is the common objective of all B's, C's, D's and F's. Everyone wants to benefit by playing someone who will hit the ball back more often than they do.

Is all this snooty stratification necessary?

Yes and no. . . . Yes, because it is obviously helpful to hit more balls against a better player. Usually the pace of his shots is quicker, which helps you develop your reflexes. Also, it's educational to discover what techniques and tactics make him a better player.

The main reason it's not always good to play up is that it becomes depressing after a while. It's like beating your head against a wall — eventually your head begins to hurt. For psychological reasons, don't always play up. Your ego and confidence may suffer.

In light of all this, the suggestion is to alternate playing *up* and *down*. For every person you play who beats you, play one you can beat.

When playing the better player, practice

132

your steadiness. Take that opportunity to see how many balls you can get back against him. Make him hit winners to beat you.

Against the inferior player, work on placement and try the shots you ordinarily wouldn't attempt in a close match. The relaxed environment will help you gain confidence. When you play someone at your own level, maybe you'll make a few. Good luck!

133

(The insurance of spin)

How to Hit Harder and Keep It in the Court

Many players haven't figured out how to increase the speed of their shots without sacrificing control.

They attempt to hit the ball harder without influencing the spin. The problem is that flat shots have a difficult time finding the court. Without the insurance of spin, the ball doesn't have enough margin of safety to be consistent.

Topspin allows the player to add more pace and yet maintain control. It is produced by a lifting motion — the racquet starts below the ball, and with the strings vertical, the ball is sent spinning end-over-end.

Underspin is the answer to topspin. It is produced by starting above the ball with the racquet, hitting down and through the ball, making it spin backwards.

Spin helps the player produce an effect with his shots — topspin for fast-dipping and high-hopping shots, underspin for slow-floating and low-bouncing shots.

Topspin is generally used for offensive purposes; underspin is used primarily for defensive reasons.

Most serves are hit with topspin — the high bounce is difficult to return and it gives the server time to get to the net. Passing shots are generally hit with topspin because the ball dips fast, sometimes at the net-player's feet.

Underspin is the natural answer to topspin — the ball leaves the racquet with the same rotation it came with, which makes it easier to control. Service returns, volleys, approach shots and lobs are often hit with underspin.

Every player must have an intellectual understanding of ball rotation, if for no other reason, so they can judge its bounce. The more experienced player should strive to influence every ball with spin, so each shot has a deliberate, planned purpose, which produces an effect, and at the same time, is hit with the confidence of knowing that it will go over the net and land inside the lines.

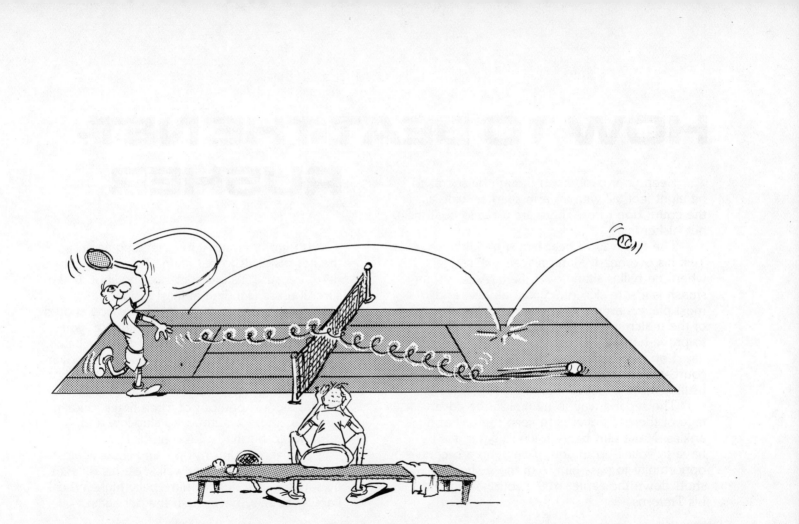

HOW TO BEAT THE NET-RUSHER

Keep your cool. Even though he seems to be eight feet tall with an arm-span as wide as the court, don't fret. There are ways to beat the net rusher.

The first way to beat him is by lobbing. Test his overhead. Many players will cringe when the ball is sitting over them. A consistent smash is a sure sign of a gifted athlete, and most players aren't. At the very beginning of the match you must give him a chance to prove himself.

Lob high and down the middle of the court. Make him retreat. A high defensive lob is usually more effective than a low offensive lob.

The second way to neutralize the advantage of the net player is to keep the ball at his ankles. Make him bend down to get it. He'll have to volley up to you, giving you a second opportunity to pass him. Aim these shoelace shots down the center of the court — right at his *Tretorns*.

A third alternative in defending against the net rusher is to pass him. This is sometimes risky, because it's an all-or-nothing shot. Make sure you are standing at least inside the baseline when you go for it. Ideally you should be closer for a good chance. Otherwise, you give him too much time to react to your ball.

Hit a majority of your passing shots down-the-line. The distance is greater and the ball gets to him faster — two things in your favor. Hit cross-court one out of three times to keep him guessing. Remember to stay low and don't try to hit the ball too hard.

Sometimes you risk passing shots against players who can't volley well. Test his reflexes by sending one right at him, belly high. Who knows, he may never rush the net again.

KNOW YOUR MARGIN OF ERROR

You are not Jimmy Connors — or Guillermo Vilas — or Evonne Goolagong — or Al Lumpwomper. You are you . . . and being you means you must play like you.

One of the problems in imitating the super stars is that their margin for error is different than yours. When you see Connors lay into one of his crunching angled service returns, you're amazed beyond belief. Not so amazed is Jimmy. He knows quite well what he is capable of. On every shot he knows his margin for error. Do you?

Two of the variables involved in hitting a tennis ball are pace and angle.

First of all, it's not smart to hit the ball so hard you can't predict where it'll go. You should set a speed limit for yourself where you're always under control.

Most excessive speed shots end up buried in the net. This is the worst way to end a point. When hitting hard you can't clear the net by much and expect it to go in — so you try a net-skimmer. And there goes your margin of error.

When you make an error caused by overhitting, realize it. Reprimand yourself by saying, "I'm not Jimmy Connors — so slow down!"

The second worst way to end a point is to hit the ball wide. This often means you were trying to be too fine, hitting a shot you haven't developed yet.

Give yourself a healthy margin for error when directing the ball. Aim as close to the line as you can without gambling. Although there are times when you can afford to be daring, usually stick with the safer, less risky shot.

In a match, stick with what you know you can do. The objective is not to allow your opponent to force you into trying shots you haven't mastered. Save those for practice. Someday you'll be able to use them in a match.

If you'll approach most of your mistakes by first analyzing these two variables, your game will improve. Most mistakes are a simple result of your: (1) trying to hit too hard, and (2) trying to be too fine. Your improper technique produces some errors, but the great majority result from either excess speed or too much angle.

HOW TO RETURN THE BIG SERVE

Are you intimidated by the big serve? Do you close your eyes, turn your head and hope you don't get hurt? You shouldn't. Here are five points that will help you develop a neutralizing service return:

(1) Position yourself on the court properly. Bisect the angle of the two widest possible serves and stand deep behind the baseline.

(2) Watch the ball as your opponent releases his service toss. See it twice: once on the toss, the second time as it bounces in front of you — *refocus* your eyes.

(3) Get your momentum going forward before he hits the ball. Time a step forward and then split-step as he tosses the ball. *Step-split-hit.* (Remember to initially position yourself deep enough to allow for this step.)

(4) Pick up your feet and move to the ball. Sometimes you'll be lucky if a leaping dive will get you to the ball; normally you'll have time to shuffle to the ball. Take two steps.

(5) Abbreviate your backswing and *borrow the power* of the ball. No swinging. Bevel the racquet back and you'll impart underspin — good for neutralizing the speed of the ball and adding control. Now you're ready for Smith's serve — that's Sally Smith, of course.

Doubles Strategy:

Improve Court Position

In the game of doubles it is unlikely you'll win many points with just one or two shots. Because the doubles court is only nine feet wider than the singles court — and there are twice as many players protecting it — the strategic plan is one of patience, placement and position. Your selection of shots should be determined with the goal of improving your court position.

First of all, be realistic when serving. If your first is not too reliable, slow down and try to place it. A medium-paced serve to the backhand will usually do the job. A deep spin serve to the backhand will make your partner look like John Newcombe at the net.

When returning serve in doubles, your goal is to keep your partner safe and out of harm's way. If you can't keep the ball low and crosscourt, your choice is either to give your partner a chest protector and a face mask, or move him back to the baseline with you.

If you have trouble handling that big serve, experiment a little. Since it's tough to hit it by them, try to dump one at the net rusher's feet. Relax your muscles when returning the ball, and sink it just over the net — right at his *Tretorns*.

After the service and the return, the objective is to improve your court position so you can get closer to the net. It's here where you can best use the angle to win the point.

In the process of working your way up to the net (shot by shot) don't make the mistake of losing your patience. You'll find too often that the alley will tease you — it just sits there, unprotected, waiting for you to try some silly non-percentage shot. Forget it! Stick to the middle of the court. Wait until you get closer to the net — then you can angle one into the alley.

Lastly, since it's tough to hit through them, try hitting over them. Lob. Choose the weakest player and make him feel like you're picking on him. If you succeed, follow your lob into the net — together. Now you're back in the right position where you have a chance to be a hero. Just wait.

COMMUNICATE...

THE HISTORIC DOUBLES DILEMMA

IN DOUBLES

One of the all-time great comedy acts in sports is played out by doubles teams everyday, everywhere. It's the old routine of "I got it! . . . I got it! . . . You take it!" The act is funny to everyone except the two partners.

Successful doubles teamwork is based on communication. Before, during, and after a point, better doubles teams talk things over.

Before the point starts, discuss tactics with your partner. If you are the receiver's partner, find out what he will do after returning serve. (You don't want to be left stranded at the net.) If he plans on staying back, you should join him before the serve is put in play.

When your partner is serving, and you believe you can poach the opponent's service return, tell him before he serves; better yet, set up a poaching signal system.

During the point, there are occasions when it is helpful to talk to your partner.

Whenever confronting a lob down the center of the court, it is best to verbally decide who will play it. Many teams will let the player with his forehand down the middle take the one in question; others let the stronger overhead play the ball. This decision should be answered with an immediate, authoritative verbal command: "MINE!" This calls the other player off the ball.

Being lobbed at the net also poses an occasional problem. Often it is easier for the *lobee's* partner to run behind him and chase down the ball. This is sensible because he has a better angle of pursuit. As he moves to the ball he tells his partner to "cross," and they change sides. At the beginning and intermediate levels of play, both players should retreat together, returning a lob with another lob.

Once at the baseline the communicating doubles team patiently waits until they are presented with an opportunity to rush the net — together. The player taking the ball should inform his partner that *they* are approaching: "Let's go!"

On the change-over (changing sides) it is time to talk about future strategy — analyze what is working and what needs to be changed. Also it is the opportune time for the partners to encourage each other and get ready for the next big game.

Doubles Strategy: Don't Play Up-and-Back; Forget the Alley

Ever stood in the doubles alley and watched your partner slug it out from the baseline?

It's the great crosscourt rally: back and forth, back and forth, back and forth . . . after a while you begin to feel like your head's on a swivel.

"I hope it doesn't come my way," you mumble to yourself, "I'd hate to ruin this point."

It's about then your opponents decide to see if you're paying attention.

Splat!!

Actually, this shouldn't be called doubles at all — but rather "alternating singles:" four players take turns playing singles on half the court while the other two make sure they don't interfere with the point.

Doubles can be a lot of fun if you make a couple of simple changes in your strategy.

The first lesson is to always play as a team. Give some respect to your partner. If he makes a mistake, try not to voice your disappointment. One nasty remark and you'll find him cringing in the doubles alley — and he's no good to you there.

Yet many doubles players spend half their lives in the alley. They stand there because their pseudo-superior partner has told them "to stay there and protect it."

Nonsense. Very few shots go down the line in doubles, so it's foolish to hang around there.

Get out in the court where the action is.

When your partner is serving, providing he can direct his serve to the backhand, move as close to the middle as you can, without getting hit in the back of the head.

By moving out in the court, you'll expose an open alley that may tempt your opponent into trying to end the point prematurely. Also, you'll put some pressure on him to make a good angled crosscourt return. (And, in the meantime, you'll develop a good volley.)

The other suggestion is to play doubles side-by-side, instead of up-and-back.

With you at the baseline and your partner at the net you expose an unprotected gap in the center of the court. If your crosscourt return doesn't make it crosscourt, your poor partner will either get nailed in his tracks or they'll casually hit the ball behind him.

The solution is to play together — either up at the net together or back at the baseline together.

If your opponent has a big serve, it's wise to move your partner back with you at the baseline; if he pushes his serve, leave your partner at the net and join him after you receive serve. If they lob, both of you retreat together.

So, to improve your doubles results, get out of the alley, don't badmouth your partner, and forget about the I formation.

DOUBLES STRATEGY: POACHING

On any given day at the courts you're bound to overhear this dialogue between doubles partners:

"I'm sorry."

"You ought to be."

"I guess it failed."

"Obviously."

"I said I'm sorry."

"Listen, from now on you cover your side of the court and I'll take care of my own. No more poaching!"

Such as it is, often this is the extent of many doubles teams' strategic plans . . . "You play your side — I'll play mine." The match usually ends up with both players taking turns playing singles on the doubles court. (Husband and wife teams call it "mixed singles.")

Poaching is fun — and profitable — but first you must have your partner's consent. Convince him (or her) by pointing out that a roving net player gives the opponents something to worry about — it makes them nervous, forcing frequent mistakes.

Once you've reached a mutual understanding, sit down and plan your poaching tactics. The first situation where the poach should be used is on the service return. Since most shots go cross court, the net player knows

committed himself, then take off in pursuit of the ball. The target of your poach should be the net player's feet. Either hit it at him or behind him. If he's playing at the base line, use your angle to put the ball away. Be aggressive — once you've made up your mind, there's no turning back.

After your first few poaches — successful or not — you should notice a tentativeness in your opponent's service returns. That's when you can employ a fake poach. Instead of actually crossing, lead them into thinking you will — and then don't. If it works, they'll send the ball at you for an easy winner.

The real effectiveness of poaching is not so much the winners that are produced but the intimidation it causes. Good doubles teams have a mutual agreement that either player can poach anytime he feels the urge. And the service return is only one poaching situation: you can intercept your partner's ball during cross court rallies, volley exchanges at the net or overheads. A poach should be made anytime one player feels he has a better chance, or a better angle at the ball. He should always be allowed to cut in front of his partner and make the play — without being cursed, threatened, or frowned upon.

right where to cut it off. If that's you, make sure your serving partner knows you're going to cross. Give him a signal before he serves (set up a system before the match). This way, he'll know to cover your vacated side (in case it doesn't work).

Timing is the most critical part of the successful poach. Wait until the receiver has

How to Return Serve in Doubles (and Earn the Respect of Your Partner)

Ever wonder why you have more trouble returning serve in doubles than in singles?

It must be due to your fear of the net player. Maybe he recently intercepted one of your floaters and tattooed it onto your partner's forehead.

Next time you play doubles try the following three "tricks" to improve your service return.

1. Before the server begins his motion, glance across the net and concentrate momentarily on the spot you'd like your return to go. Be realistic. Choose an area near the service line, crosscourt, away from the net player. Don't be impatient if you miss; keep concentrating. The power of positive thinking always produces results.

2. Move in a step and take the ball as it rises. This is good preventative medicine, especially for the backhand service return. It will make it easier for you to keep the ball low. Take a step or two inside the baseline and, with the racquet beveled back, catch the ball early, about chest level. Keep a firm wrist and the racquet head high.

3. Relax. Some shots involve more muscles than others. For example, a forehand volley requires more energy than a drop shot. One ball leaves the racquet quickly, the other slowly. The objective of the service return in doubles is to keep the ball low enough so the volleyer has to pop it up, so you get a chance to pass him. This is easier to accomplish if you hit the ball softly, by relaxing your shoulder, arm, and grip. Not only are you more accurate, but the slow speed of your return is tough to handle for the net-charging server.

Keep these three suggestions in mind next time your partner looks back at you with ink on his forehead. He'll appreciate it.

How to Follow Your Into the Net

Occasionally when running up to net you'll meet one of those beautiful low-flying lobs — the kind that appear bigger than life, too good to be true. Boom! Everyone scatters for safety.

Other times you charge forward, looking for another setup, only to stumble past the ball. An awkward lunge, a desperate stab, and you come up with nothing but embarrassment.

Following your serve or an approach shot

into net is tricky business. You have to be careful not to overrun the return. If you're moving forward as the ball is being hit, it becomes difficult to move laterally for the wide shots.

Smart tennis players seldom run to the net at full blast — they move forward with haste but under control, with poise and balance. It depends on the individual skill of the player to determine how quickly he can move without becoming clumsy with his shot-making. One player may run with poise at 20 miles per hour while another might have to slow down to 5 m.p.h.

If you are an aspiring serve-and-volleyer, it's helpful to evaluate your footwork. The first step into the court, for the right hander, should be with the right foot. Except for big flat serves, you'll have time to take two more steps before doing a "split-stop." This simple hopscotch step is executed by spreading your feet wide, stopping with both feet gripping the court simultaneously. Try to land on your toes, instead of your heels. If the ground shakes when you split-stop, better lighten up and practice more.

By the time you split-stop you should notice where the return is headed. If it's dipping low toward your feet, stop dead in your tracks, bend, and scoop up the ball; if it's a floater, you'll want to take a couple of quick steps forward to intercept the ball closer to the net.

The split-stop is frequently omitted by many aggressive, but reckless, players. After serving the ball they simply charge the net, elbows flying, knees kicking — out of control. If the return isn't high and down the middle, they get in trouble.

To monitor your poise and balance, be deliberate with every step. During your practice matches say to yourself: "Right . . . left . . . right . . . split." Volley with your front foot flat on the ground, knee bent.

The split-stop is also needed following an approach shot. Again, the timing of the stop is critical. It must take place before the ball is hit; it doesn't matter where you are on the court — even if you got a late start coming in on a deep ball, and you're still in no-man's-land, split-stop anyway. Play the ball, move forward, and split-stop again.

The split-stop is used in all situations where lateral movement is anticipated. That includes the service return. When your opponent drops his hands down to initiate his serve, take a step forward, then split-stop. You'll find it easier to reach those wide slice serves.

HOW TO THINK YOUR SERVE IN

When you blow an easy shot on a crucial point, do you find yourself thinking out loud:

". . . How could I miss that shot? I had the whole court! When am I ever going to stop choking on big points? Now the score is 15-30, instead of 30-15. If I lose the next point, and I probably will, the score will be 15-40 which all but eliminates my chances of winning the game. That'll make the set score 3-4, and if he wins his serve, the score will be 3-5, which most likely will cost me the set and more than likely the match, which is not all bad except that I hate this guy because he'll tell everyone he beat me. . . ."

These gloomy predictions will all come true if you spend your time forecasting them. Instead of brooding over a mistake, spend the following 30 seconds planning the next point. You have several decisions to make and if you spend that critical time trying to figure out why you're such a loser, you won't give yourself a chance to be a winner.

Be positive in your approach to mistakes. Think of what you could have done better, rather than what went wrong; then immediately start preparing for the next point. Slowly walk back to the baseline so you have time to collect your thoughts.

The serve is the most crucial part of tennis. The entire act represents your determination and confidence. In it you dictate the tempo of the match. You are the decision maker. The percentage of first-serves-in demonstrates your ability to concentrate and succeed. Before you toss the ball, decide: where you will hit it, how hard you will hit it, and what you will do after you hit it. In your mind's eye you see the serve go where you want. You think it in. Serve only when you're ready — after you've "seen" it go there.

Learning to be positive and concentrate is a never-ending process. You develop this part of your game in the same way you improve your strokes. You must practice. Today you may react negatively to 90 per cent of your mistakes. It's unrealistic to expect that tomorrow you'll be able to play nonjudgmental tennis like Bjorn Borg or Chris Evert; you can, however, improve little by little.

The first step is to stop talking to yourself. "Thoughts take force when they are pronounced." So be quiet. Be deliberate. Don't serve until you've seen the result. Plan the point. Be positive and think success.

The Story of King Kong's Pathetic Serve (And How It Relates to You)

King Kong had the world's most pathetic serve. As strong as he was, Kong was never able to hit the ball faster than 18 miles an hour. When he followed it into the net, you could almost knock it down his throat.

The problem with Mr. Kong's serve was his overpowering strength — he couldn't relax. As he dropped the racquet behind his back, he squeezed the grip so tight he made sawdust. He couldn't seem to understand that to hit a forceful serve you don't have to force it.

Somebody once said aptly that you must *"let the serve serve itself."* The server's responsibility is just to start it properly.

Most everyone is familiar with the path the racquet head should take. Some pattern it after a figure-8 or a lasso throw. There's supposed to be a loop behind the back that has something to do with rhythm and potential power.

If you make it through this magical pattern, you're guaranteed a good serve. But try as you can, you (and Kong) can't get the feel of this loop. All you can manage is a semi-loop — a grunt — and a push.

Try the *three finger serve*. This promises to cure all "cement-mixer" arms. Hold the knob-end of the racquet with your forefinger, middle-finger and thumb. Pretend the racquet is the pendulum of a grandfather clock. Relax your arm. Make it seem like jello or spaghetti; let it dangle from your side. Now sweep the racquet-head through the motion without the ball. Can you feel the weight of the pendulum? After 15 practice swings, try hitting a ball. Instead of using the court, hit it into a fence or backboard. (If you try too hard to get the ball in the court, you may regress to your cement-mixer serve.)

Be loose and sloppy. Let the racquet head sink down behind your back and reach up to flop over the ball. (You may have to extend your service toss higher.)

After you get the feel of the three finger serve, try four fingers for a while. Leave your baby finger off the grip.

Later you can use all five fingers as you think how it felt with three. Be loose as a goose. . . .

(In case you're interested, Godzilla did not play tennis.)

Change Tactics for Emergency Shots

Tennis players often put too much emphasis on the power shots and not enough on how to return them.

When your opponent hits a ball that sends you reeling back to the fence, the only answer you can make consistently is a lob. If you're 85 to 90 feet from his baseline, and leaning backwards, send it up in the air — deep.

Another shot which regularly puts tennis players in bad humor is the short ball — the one which sends you sprinting into the court, only to dribble it into the net, or knock it over the baseline.

The secret here is to hit down through the ball with the racquet beveled back. The angle of the racquet face will get the ball over the net, and the stroke will keep it in the court.

Another time in tennis you need a defensive shot is when your opponent sends you scrambling wide, off the court. Don't think you're doomed and try for the all-or-nothing shot. (This is how most balls are lost.)

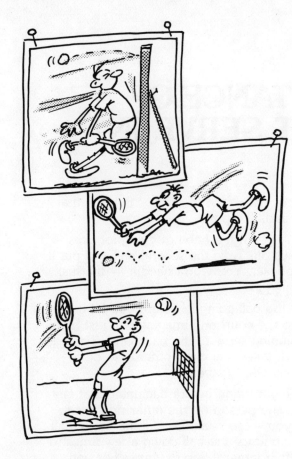

When both players are back at the baseline, wide shots should be hit high over the net, and crosscourt. If your opponent is at the net, and you're behind the baseline, lob.

Big booming serves can be returned by simply blocking the ball with the racquet beveled back. No backswing, no followthrough.

In all these emergency situations, a good general rule is to send the ball down the center of the court. It doesn't make sense to hit wide, because your goal is just to keep it in play.

Mistakes in tennis always outnumber winners. Lob, chip, dive and scramble to get the ball back. Give him another opportunity to miss.

"Good shot!"

REALIZE THE IMPORTANCE OF GETTING YOUR FIRST SERVE IN

During the analysis of one student's videotaping we noticed that as his racquet was stretched overhead to make contact with the first ball, his left hand was in his pocket digging out the second.

Tournament players place an enormous amount of importance on getting the first serve in play. It's easy to see why.

In a statistical study of a recent Stan Smith - John Newcombe match, it was found if the players got their first serve in, their chances of winning the point were 67 percent. However, if they missed the first one, their chances dropped to 53 percent.

Many club level players foolishly consider the first serve as a free opportunity to try for an ace. Their second serve is the one that actually starts the point.

Don't get in the habit of trying for aces — it never pays off. Take the second ball and put it in your pocket. You won't need it — the first one is going in.

See the ball going in before you hit it. Look into the court and imagine you just hit a deep, spinning serve to the backhand. Then do just that. It takes real concentration to be a consistently good player.

Take your time before beginning that first delivery. The person on the other side has to wait for you — so relax. Be like the basketball player — bounce the ball down a few times to set the environment. Say to yourself as you bounce the ball four times, "I-can-make-it." By bouncing the ball before serving you are helping make *every* serve like the one before.

Start your motion on balance and relaxed. Don't serve until you are ready. Make sure you are totally relaxed as you line up your feet, shoulders, arms and racquet. Consciously make your muscles loose and limp. Think jello before you (slowly) begin the motion.

If, by some freak accident, you happen to miss the first serve, take the same deliberate steps for the second one. There is no such thing as a second serve, so don't treat it any differently. Just hit another first one with a bit more spin.

Remember, you'll never double fault if you always get the first serve in play.

UNDERHIT YOUR OVERHEAD

Many a deafening scream has been aired following the act of hitting an overhead smash. All that energy, all that power, all that anxious anticipation.

And there lies the ball, innocently, at the foot of the net. How did it get there?

You over-hit another overhead.

Overheads are easy to miss if you try too hard; they're just like every other shot in this game — if you try to hit them harder than you're able, you'll miss more than you make. (Oh, but you want to cream it — make it one shot the fans will never forget?)

Don't settle for just one good shot. Put all your overheads away — into the court.

The secret to smashing success is controlling your body at the moment of truth. Two basic mistakes cause most overhead disasters: one is pulling your head down just before the point of contact (to hopefully see the ball land in the court), and the other is to throw your hips back in a jackknife position, letting the ball drop too low. The combination of these two errors in technique predictably sends the ball into the net.

The next time you practice your overhead, try the following three remedies to your embarrassing problem.

The first clue is to keep your chin up until after you have hit the ball. Get in the habit of looking at the spot where you just made contact. Instead of dropping your head as you try to hit down, say to yourself, "Chin up, hit down."

The second clue is to bend your front knee. Move your feet quickly so you can take a long stride forward. Bending your front knee will help stabilize your balance, helping you control your muscles to make a consistent centerhit. After contact, momentarily hold your finish, making sure you have flexed the front knee.

The third tip is to hit your overhead only as hard as you can control your body. Don't try to scare anybody. Be deliberate and try to direct the ball. Since you are at the net, take advantage of the potential angle. A not-too-hard, carefully hit, well-placed overhead is exciting.

And, instead of screaming, you get to smile.

How to Play the Sunday Slugger

Ever let your ego get involved in a slugfest rally from the baseline?

Like a couple of unskilled boxers — each of you tries to knock the other out with one punch.

When you go on the court against a slugger, you must realize that he is going to determine the fate of almost every point. He's either going to win the point, via a putaway, or he's going to lose it by making an error. Your goal is obvious: get the ball back until he misses.

To help you accomplish that goal, take advantage of the fact that it's difficult to create pace — when the ball comes slowly it requires precise timing to send it fast.

So, instead of returning pace with pace, return it with no pace. Float the ball back softly, high over the net, and deep. Use underspin to slow the ball's flight.

Many aggressive hitters have difficulties near the net. They relish chasing you from corner to corner — from the baseline their shots have depth and authority, but from mid-court or the net the story might be different. They may lack the finesse required to keep the ball in the court.

Feed these players soft, short-angled, underspin dink shots. If they come in, pass or lob; if they retreat, hit a deep ball to a corner.

Both these suggestions are dependent on your ability to control the pace and spin of the ball. If you're just a beginner, and big hitters still scare the heck out of you, then it's premature to expect you'll be able to do much with the ball. You can, however, learn not to back up, fall away or close your eyes when the ball is flying in your direction.

Lean forward. Bevel the racquet face back and chip the ball with underspin.

This might be confusing: when the ball comes slowly you should move backwards, playing the ball as it descends, but when it

comes screaming
across the net,
keep your
ground and
block it
back. Got it?
The last tip is
for all levels
of play: If you
anticipate that your
big-hitting opponent is
going to rip one in the
corner, don't stand there
in the middle of the court,
hoping he misses.

The chances of him making a mistake
increase when he expects you'll make the
return. The pressure rises with every ball you
struggle to get back; he knows he can't make
many low-percentage shots in a row.

Let him know you're scrambling and not
spectating.

165

HOW TO COMBAT THE JITTERS

Do you get violent in a match? Many people are great ralliers but can't play when it counts. They get too emotional.

Tennis is a difficult game to play when overly excited. Your body doesn't respond. Although your head knows what to do, your obstinate arms and legs won't listen.

Is it possible to force yourself to relax and keep your poise? Sure it is. Athletes in all sports have subtle tricks to remind themselves to stay relaxed. Here are some things you can do to relax and play up to your potential in tennis.

(1) **Don't serve the ball until you are ready.** Your opponent can't do anything until you serve the ball, so take your time. Calm yourself by bouncing the ball a few times before starting. Take a deep breath and think the ball to the target.

(2) **Relax your grip.** A *sawdust grip* is a major cause of tennis elbow and a characteristic of a nervous game. When serving check to see that you are allowing the grip to breathe. During the point you can develop the automatic reflex of turning the racquet once in your hand between shots.

(3) **Relax your legs.** A tennis player bounces between shots. After he hits the ball, he recovers his court position and bounces gracefully on the balls of his feet. This action reminds him to relax and helps his mobility.

(4) **Shrug your shoulders.** Before serving and returning serve, check your nervousness by relaxing your shoulders and neck. Think jello.

(5) **Don't watch your opponent.** Don't become paranoid anticipating your opponent's next move. Many inexperienced players habitually take their eyes off the ball to see where their opponent is. Watch the ball!

HELPING THE "HEAD CASE"

"My mind is so fickle. Sometimes, when I concentrate well, nobody is too tough for me; other times, when I'm playing poorly I can't even keep track of the score."

Concentration means different things to different people. Most players agree that sticking to the subject at hand is what keeps them in the match; others swear they play best while their mind is off somewhere else.

Usually this state of "unconsciousness" occurs when you're playing against either an inferior opponent or someone who's appreciably better. In either case, there is no pressure on you to make the shots — so you relax, your muscles respond beautifully, and you play better than ever. Unfortunately, this relaxed, fluid feeling turns to granite when playing in a tight match. It's this situation where your concentration begins to slip.

Learning to concentrate properly takes self-discipline and hard work. It's a skill to be acquired — just like your forehand or backhand. For some it comes naturally — others have to work at it. Everyone can improve.

A healthy, positive approach helps tremendously. If you think you're going to lose, it's difficult to put yourself in the proper frame of mind to compete. The problem may be you're afraid of losing the war while still fighting the battle. You are not thinking in the present — you're not playing one point at a time.

Have you noticed the pros bounce the ball a few times before serving? It's here where they plan their attack for the point.

Placing a great deal of importance on their serve, they make sure to start the point in their advantage. This is why they concentrate so hard before tossing it up.

They plan their attack. The first decision is where to direct the serve and how hard to hit it. They actually see the serve before releasing the toss. They have foresight. In their mind's eye they complete the desired motion. They concentrate.

Concentration also means looking ahead in the point — anticipating. If you plan on hitting a big serve, predict a weak return. If you expect your opponent to crunch one of your weak second serves, quickly take a step or two back, anticipating a deep shot. Most players fall into predictable patterns of play. It is your responsibility to determine what they are. Where does he serve? Where does he return your various serves? Where does he approach? When does he lob? Where does he like to pass? Concentrate.

Lastly, concentration means making positive errors. When you (eventually) miss, learn something from your mistake. See yourself making the shot you just missed. Actually walk through the correct stroke. Relive the play, this time making the shot. Be positive and concentrate.

THE SLICE SERVE MAKES YOU VERSATILE

Most everyone agrees the strategic objective of the serve is to make the opponent play a backhand. This often becomes such a challenging goal that many players forget to try anything else.

Clever players, however, derive great joy from sending an occasional, sneaky *slice* serve wide to the forehand. This often catches the receiver off balance, setting up a weak return.

To learn the slice serve you must first make sure you are using the proper service grip. Your palm should rest on the top right bevel of the handle, halfway between the forehand and backhand grips.

As you first learn the slice serve, it may be easier if you toss the ball farther to your right than usual. On your first few attempts toss the ball a foot or more to the right. Contact the side of the ball, imparting sidespin. This is easier if you visualize the ball as a clock. Hit the ball at 2:35.

Properly executed, the ball should hook to your left, bouncing away from your opponent. Practice until you can control its direction.

You'll discover the slice serve is most effective on the deuce court. Its wide bounce sends your opponent reaching off the court. If all goes right, you'll have an open court and a chance for a winner.

Sometimes the slice serve is suicidal. If you don't hit it correctly, you give your opponent an easy shot to his strength. It's like throwing a curveball that doesn't break. This is bound to happen occasionally. Don't fret. Not every shot can be a winner. Even though you may lose a few points this way, the fact that you are a threat going to your opponent's forehand will make your serve to the backhand more effective. You'll see . . .

Teach Yourself TOPSPIN

If you could own one spectacular shot in tennis, what would it be?

A deftly disguised drop shot? A Roscoe Tanner serve? A crunching backpedal overhead?

The last person asked said he always dreamed of having a topspin lob.

It's a good choice. There's no shot in tennis more exciting or surprising than a topspin lob.

And you can learn one. In fact, anyone can.

It just takes years.

To begin to learn a topspin lob, teach yourself how to hit a topspin forehand.

Find a practice partner — someone who shares your aspirations. Stand on opposite sides of the net, at the service lines. Draw your racquet back as you prepare to bounce-hit the ball to him. Glance behind you and slightly "close" (turn downwards) the face of the

racquet. Gently toss the ball about shoulder high in front of your left foot; start below the ball with the racquet, and lift it over the net. Watch it travel: check to see if it's spinning end over end.

Instead of returning the ball, your partner should catch it and repeat the same procedure.

The next time you try it, hold your followthrough position; you should have a clear view over the top of your elbow, your hand should be at the level of your eyes, racquet pointed straight up in the sky.

Later, when you're both confidently hitting topspin, instruct your partner to bevel back the racquet face and, instead of catching the ball, return it with underspin. Play the ball back with topspin, instructing him to catch it. Then he'll start the rally and it'll be your turn to underspin it. (That's topspin, underspin, topspin, catch.)

Eventually, move back to the baseline and continue this drill.

After still more practice, try to keep the rally going — one topspinning, the other underspinning.

If your topspin stops spinning, catch the ball, take your racquet back, close it, bounce the ball in front, start low, and lift it over the net.

You'll discover that a topspin forehand is easier to hit when the ball is coming slowly, with a high bounce. This gives you time and room to get your racquet below the ball.

After you learn a topspin forehand, your next goal is to incorporate the shot into a point.

The best shot from the baseline is a looping topspin forehand, hit high and deep to the opponent's backhand. Or you can use topspin as a passing shot — the ball dips down at the net player's feet.

And, of course, there's the topspin lob. Can't you just see it now?

173

KNOW THE CRITICAL POINTS IN TENNIS

The following hilarious exchange was recently overheard on the courts between two obliging club-level tennis players:

"What's the score?" asked the server as he stood on the 'ad' court.

"It's either 30-15 or 15-30," answered his equally confused opponent.

"Shall we play deuce?" questioned the server.

"Go ahead," he agreed.

And so they continued play at *deuce* on the *ad* court.

During the course of a match you may find yourself thinking about everything else but what is at hand. Perhaps you also find it difficult to keep track of the score.

In tennis there are critical times when you cannot afford one of these mental blackouts. It is during these momentous occasions that you must gather your wits, force yourself to concentrate and try as hard as you can.

For instance, try to win the first point of the game. This gives you an important psychological *edge* over your opponent.In a recent WCT professional tournament, the author statistically discovered that the server had an almost unbelievable 90 per cent chance of winning the game if he won the first point. If he lost it, his chances dropped to 64 per cent.

The third point is also critical. It is a psychological turning point that you must win. You either fall decisively behind or give yourself a substantial lead.

In the final match of the tournament, between John Newcombe and Stan Smith, the server had a 95 per cent chance of winning the game if he won the third point. If he lost it, his chances plunged to 29 per cent.

At the set level, it is important to concentrate on the first game. A psychological *edge* here may be all you need.

The seventh game is also special. The score will be 5-1, 4-2, 3-all, 2-4 or 1-5. If the score is close and you win this game, chances are you will win the set.

Besides concentrating on these critical points and games, you must learn what to do when you play them. The experienced player tries to work his favorite play. As the baseball pitcher relies on his best pitch when he is in a jam, so does the tennis player put together a combination of his favorite shots.

For example, you may have great success serving wide to the backhand, on the ad court, and putting away a forehand volley (if the return is weak). This may be your favorite *1-2 combination*. Use it when you need the big point.

Perhaps your greatest strength lies in your baseline consistency. If so, when things get nervous, stay back and slug it out. Whatever your preference, try to position yourself so you are comfortable and can hit your favorite shot.

An intelligent suggestion from the pros is always to make the percentage shot on these critical points. Don't gamble. On the *unimportant* points (like 40-15 or 40-0) they may choose a riskier, nonpercentage shot. This helps make their percentage shots more effective.

Scoring in tennis is complicated. The individual points are not weighted the same. Some points are worth more — psychologically. Know which ones are and get tough!

STRATEGY FOR THE SERVE

Contrary to how it sometimes appears, the objective of the serve in tennis is to start the point, not finish it.

Instead of trying for an "ace," inexperienced players should approach every serve as an opportunity to practice the proper technique and just place the ball in the court.

By slowing the delivery, concentrating, and keeping his balance, before long his confidence will grow to the point where he'll be able to direct the ball.

Next, the tactic should be to expose a weakness — usually the backhand.

To assist in this tactic, it is helpful to position yourself properly on the court. When serving into the deuce (right) court, stand as close to the center service mark as possible (when serving to another right-hander). On the ad court, move over six feet to get a better angle at the backhand.

Eventually the player must add some imagination to his serve. He should perfect a slice serve — one that pulls his opponent wide to his forehand.

Now the server can be clever. He can begin the point by putting his opponent on the defensive; he starts the point first by deciding which plan to use.

176

Baseline players generally like to keep their service placements wide; properly executed, this tactic opens up the court for the following shot.

The third tactic in serving is to handcuff the opponent by serving right at him. This can be done by aiming the slice serve at his backhand. Hopefully, the ball will slide right into his belly. (Watch for a short return.)

The most important strategic lesson in serving concerns the second serve. Although you want to make sure you don't double fault, it's absolutely against the unwritten rules of good tennis to push your second serve into play.

A blooper-ball serve is a sure sign of a hacker, and if you're going to master this game you must accept the challenge of hitting your second serve.

The only way to stop lobbing your second serve is to stop lobbing it. Hit the ball with the same technique as your first, just compromise a little speed for some more spin.

HOW TO GET MAXIMUM EXTENSION ON THE SERVE

Pretend you are seven feet tall. With your racquet you could reach ten feet in the air. Imagine the serve you would have. When you walked on the court grown men would cringe; little children would run and hide. You would be feared by all.

Now quit daydreaming. Unfortunately, you are not seven feet tall and you have to make the most of what you have. You must take full advantage of your maximum height.

Don't sit down on your serve. Many players lose valuable height because they hunch over as they make contact. You must be at least as tall as you are when hitting the ball.

Unless you have the opportunity to see yourself on videotape, it is difficult to tell whether you are taking advantage of your height. It is suggested that you practice the following drills to check your technique and emphasize the correct motion.

First check your service toss. It's possible that by tossing the ball too low you will limit your reach. Try this drill: toss the ball and touch your back with the racquet before you hit it. If you find the ball has dropped before you can reach up to make contact, you may need extra height on your toss.

Now check the position of your toss. Many inexperienced players toss the ball so far in front they have to chase it to make contact. By the time they reach the ball it has dropped to the level of their chest. A mighty groan and

hefty swat result in nothing more than another fault into the bottom of the net.

You should be able to hit your biggest serve from a balanced position. No stepping, jumping, or leaping. For the moment, don't rise on your front toes. Stay flat footed. Serve and hold your finish. Try tossing the ball over your forehead and stretch up to hit it. A balanced serve means a coordinated service toss.

The following drill will check your extension at the point of contact. Hit a few serves in slow motion. Make everything rhythmical and fluid.

After you get the feel of the slowed-down motion, try stopping the racquet head at the point of contact position. Freeze! Check this position. Your arm should be extended to full reach overhead. A straight line is formed from your racquet to your left foot.

Keep your chin up throughout the motion. Gradually speed up the serve, driving up and through the ball. Watch the point of contact even after the ball is gone.

Think of your service motion as if you were on a stepladder trying to reach up as high as you can. And remember: perfect practice makes perfect.

179

The Chip
Service Return

During his prime, Pancho Gonzales was renowned for having two of the greatest shots in tennis — the serve and the service-return. By concentrating on these two shots, Gonzales was able to stay atop the professional tennis ladder for many years.

Although many tournament players can regularly hold serve, it's the exceptional player who can break serve with any frequency.

Gonzales' service-return accuracy was amazing. At this level of competition it is critical to keep the ball low, so the net-rushing server can't take advantage of the wide angled shots at the net. Pancho would neutralize the offensive potential of the server by consistently dropping the ball at his feet, forcing him to defensively volley the ball from below the net.

To accomplish this precise placement of the ball, he made effective use of underspin. This produced a more conservative hit, yet one in which he could dictate the very spot he had in mind.

Much of your success in returning serve is dependent on reflexes. Against the big server all the action takes place in less than a split second. You have to read the direction of the serve, turn your shoulders, change grips (if necessary), and move forward to intercept the ball. There's little time to fool around.

The main key to this reflex shot may be the quick pivot of the shoulders; after all, there's hardly time to move the feet when the ball is approaching at 100 mph.

The technique of the service return is similar to that of the volley. The racquet face is beveled back as it hits the bottom of the ball, imparting underspin. Backswing and followthrough are minimal. In attempting to learn this shot, try dropping your front shoulder an inch or two so you don't sail the ball over the fence. You may have to experiment until you discover exactly how much bevel is needed to produce the desired effect.

Another important ingredient in the service return is your forward movement into the ball. Instead of allowing the ball to come to you, move forward to intercept it. Play the ball as it is rising, or at the top of its bounce. To absorb the extra speed of the ball, maintain a firm wrist and keep the racquet head up.

At first it may be difficult for you to catch the ball as it rises, especially if you are an inexperienced player (in which case you shouldn't try it). You can, however, learn to move forward and into the shot. Try standing back farther than usual and take a step forward as the server swings up at the ball. Just as the ball is hit do a *split stop:* spread your feet wide and land on your toes. *Step and split.* This will help keep your upper body forward, which should contribute to a consistent, low hit at the net-rusher's ankles. Along with a quick and complete shoulder turn, you should be on your way to developing a Pancho Gonzales service-return.

WHAT TO DO WHEN YOU'RE LOSING

(But Haven't Lost Yet)

Don't get mad. I know you're frustrated with yourself. It's embarrassing to be beaten this way. And what makes it worse is that you should be on top of this guy. Somehow you have to get control of yourself and turn this thing around.

The first step is to stop hating yourself. This is only making you tighter. Plus it is giving your opponent an unfair psychological advantage. He can see you're distraught and it is making him feel better and better.

Instead of wrinkling up your face every time you lose a point, smile. Constant grumblings and mutterings only make you more depressed. "Thoughts take force when they are pronounced." So don't utter negative thoughts. Keep them to yourself. When he hits a nice shot say, "Nice shot." When you flub an easy set-up promise yourself, "Next time I'll put it away."

The second experimental step to remedy your losing game is slowing down. The key is to quiet your body, relax your arm, unclench your grip, and get your "feel" back. This is best accomplished by slowing the pace of your shots. Hit only soft balls. Loosen your muscles and be rhythmical. In the ready position release your grip on the racquet by holding it in your left hand. Stand straight from the waist. (Don't hunch over like a football player.) Bounce rhythmically on your toes. Exaggerate your followthrough. Be cool.

Your objective is to play your way back into form. By relaxing, you may recover your strokes and their effectiveness.

If you're still getting pushed around, take a look at your opponent's game and see what he is feeding on. Whatever it is, don't give him any more.

You must change a losing game. This also means you must prevent your opponent from playing his winning game. First of all, you should take away his favorite shot. Give him anything but what he likes. If he loves fast balls, send him slow underspinning floaters. If he likes to rally from the baseline, bring him into the net and make him volley. If he likes to hit big forehands, send nothing but wide angles to his backhand, if his overhead is suspect, bombard him with lobs. Instead of playing your regular game for awhile, do whatever it takes to upset his.

Remember, a psychological edge determines the outcome of most tennis matches. And the difference between being "psyched up" and "psyched out" is very subtle.

IS "CHOKING" INCURABLE?

Contrary to popular belief, *choking* (e.g. double-faulting on match point) is not terminal. Although some players suffer their entire career, others work hard at curing this malady.

The only way to tame match-point jitters is to play a lotta match points. Here are some suggestions.

(1) Play as many different players as possible. Seek them out in tournaments, challenge matches, pick-up matches, etc. Continually facing the new and unexpected will

help make you more perceptive and mentally stronger.

(2) Play some practice matches where you allow yourself only one serve to put the ball in play. This extra pressure will make you tougher — and will help you learn the importance of getting the first serve in.

(3) Play some practice matches using the VASS scoring system (ping pong). Bet 10 cents on each point and play to 31. The added pressure should make you nervous. (Try playing tie-breakers at 50 cents.)

(4) Play *handicap matches* against your regular partners. If someone consistently wins by a predictable score, determine a fair number of games to give the loser before the match begins. If you always win 6-3 or 6-4, next time start the match trailing 0-2. Put the pressure on.

If you put yourself in the jittery situation often, you're bound to have success sometime. Eventually, your confidence will grow and you won't turn *belly up* so often.

How to Improve By Watching Better Players

If you want to be a good player you have to be a good student, and to be a good student you have to be a good spectator.

Learning is watching.

Many people aspire to be better tennis players but lack the patience to sit and watch. They'd rather do it themselves, even though realizing they're not doing it correctly.

If you would like to give your game a boost, pick a stroke or fundamental that needs improvement and go to work.

The initial step is to find someone who excels at what you would like to, then spend some time watching him or her.

Sit behind the player and focus your attention on him. Concentrate. Ignore the ball. When the action stops, close your eyes and repeat what you just saw with them open.

Throughout the day, at school, the office or home, close your eyes and treat yourself to a repeat performance. Whenever you have a spare moment, review what you saw. Also, when it's convenient, take your racquet out and mimic what you have been seeing in your mind. Pretend you are the player you're emulating.

Back on the tennis court, try your best to imitate your teacher. Do everything he does except hit the ball as hard. (Since you will probably pick a person who has more playing experience than you, it is likely he will have the ability to hit the ball with more pace, yet still maintain control. Do what he does, but at your own speed.)

You may have to schedule quite a few spectating sessions before you start to catch on; then you'll have to spend time on the court practicing. It may take a month, or two, or three, before you assume the characteristics of your master teacher.

Be patient. Watch. Think. Pretend. And keep practicing.

How to Make Intelligent Mistakes

Intelligent tennis players make intelligent mistakes.

You can finish a point by hitting short, wide or long, crosscourt or down the line. Where it goes demonstrates your strategy or lack thereof.

In baseline rallies your objective is to keep your opponent away from the net. The farther back he is forced to play the ball, the smaller an angle he has to work with (and the shorter he's apt to return it). Your objective is to hit the ball deep.

If, in your attempt to hit deep, you send the ball into the net, consider that a "dumb mistake." It's not consistent with your objective. It doesn't make sense. Miss deep.

Only miss wide when trying for an angle; and only try for an angle when standing inside your baseline.

Your objective when rushing the net is to play the ball deep, putting your opponent in a defensive position. Again, if your miss, miss long.

At the net your strategy is to keep the ball deep enough so your opponent doesn't have an angle to pass you. Press his backhand side until he sends a soft return, then step forward and angle it away for a winner.

When defending against the net-rusher, your alternatives are passing, lobbing or chipping short. Your selection depends on your opponent, his approach shot and your skills.

If you're forced back by a penetrating volley or approach shot, lob. Once in a while chip a soft crosscourt near the service line; it may catch him moving back, anticipating another lob.

If he hits short you have an opportunity to pass. Hit down the line more often than crosscourt. Keep the ball low, but don't over-hit it. (Here's a situation where your mistake can be short, wide or long — all intelligent!)

When serving, your goal is normally to hit the ball deep and to a corner. You can miss wide or long, but never in the net.

When receiving serve it depends on your opponent's strategy to determine your answer: if he follows it in, chip softly at his feet (it's okay to occasionally hit the net); if he stays back at the baseline, your strategy is to make him move back to play a backhand (it's not okay to hit the net).

For most players, mistakes outnumber winners by at least 10-1; it's how you miss that determines your future improvement. Make mistakes that make sense.

HOW TO PLAY "PERCENTAGE TENNIS"

Of the many reasons people play tennis, probably the No. 1 reason is to win.

Playing tennis to win is different from playing tennis for recreation. When playing to win you need a game plan.

Most mature players follow a plan which is commonly referred to as "percentage tennis." It means hitting the most *effective* shot with a comfortable margin of error — one that makes it easy to cover the opponent's return. It's what you "should" do on the court.

Following are most of the playing situations in tennis and the suggested "percentage shots."

In serving, the percentage shot is directed to the opponent's backhand. When returning serve, against the baseline player, the objective is to make the server move back to play a backhand. If he follows his serve to net, the smart shot is a soft, low, short return down the middle, at his feet. Your intention is to force him to pop the ball up so you can pass him.

The percentage shot in a baseline rally is crosscourt: the net is lower, the court longer, and the distance to recover not as great. High deep shots, landing at least six feet from the side and baseline are ideal for this playing situation.

When approaching the net, percentage tennis dictates you go deep, down-the-line. It's easier to get in position to cover the widest of possible returns.

When you make it to the net, the logical volley is to the open court: if your opponent attempts to pass you down-the-line, volley crosscourt. Deep volleys that pass the service line are valued.

When defending against the net rusher, it depends on your opponent's approach shot or volley to determine your answer. If he plays the ball deep, so you're forced to return it from a position behind the baseline, the percentage shot is a lob, over his backhand. If his short shot brings you inside the baseline, your passing shot should be directed down-the-line: the ball reaches the net player quicker, and the distance for the ball to travel is greater.

Every player has personal pet shots he loves to hit. There may be high risk involved, but he feels it's worth it. If you can't resist trying tricky drop shots, wide slice serves or crosscourt passing shots, at least make sure you attempt them on "unimportant" points. Wait until you get ahead 40-love or 40-15, then you can entertain your creativity.

191

DISCOVER THE ANGLES IN TENNIS

Professional tennis is exciting to watch. It's impressive to watch the pro hit the ball so hard his opponent can't get his racquet on it. Aces, passing shots and crisp volley winners bring the crowd to its feet. Like the long touchdown pass

— one play and it's all over.

Back on the home courts, the impressionable fan has a tough time impressing anyone. His power shots either end up in the net or against the fence. Try as he will, he can't seem to hit the ball past his opponent.

An intelligent alternative to power tactics is to direct the ball and make use of angles. This takes a different kind of playing personality. Instead of being impulsive, the player must learn to be patient.

The serve is your first opportunity to direct the ball. Your choice is to slice it wide, serve down the middle, or hit directly at your opponent. In order to pinpoint your serve, take something off the speed — sacrifice a little steam for some direction.

After putting the ball in play, most of your shots should land deep in the court, at least behind the service line. Aim high over the net. Wait until your opponent hits a shorter ball, one that you play from inside the baseline, then take advantage of the cross-court angle.

To learn angle shots, practice them during baseline rallies and warmups. Instead of exchanging hits down the middle of the court, rally cross-court or down-the-line. Practice the shots you need for the match.

In the tedious progression of developing a better game, a considerable time is spent hitting the ball right back to your opponent. He's like a magnet — every shot returns to him. In a rally you instinctively know your best chance of keeping the ball in the court is to hit it back where it came from. You hesitate to risk changing the angle of the ball. Someday, however, you must be daring and take that risk. When it isn't coming too hard, try hitting it where he isn't. A good way to practice these new shots is to play a game called *Crosscourt-down-the-line.*

From the baseline, play all your shots down-the-line; your opponent returns them all cross-court. (Start the point hitting a forehand dtl; he returns a backhand cc; you hit back dtl; and he plays a forehand cc . . . etc.) Keep score ping-pong style; play until one gets 11 points, then switch shots (you hit cross-court, he returns down-the-line).

Most points in tennis are lost. Many are lost because of forced mistakes. These are produced by moving the opponent around until he loses his poise and commits an error. To force your opponents into more errors, be patient and make use of court angles. You'll discover it's easier than hitting it by them.

THINK YOURSELF TO BETTER TENNIS

Close your eyes and picture this: You're smooth as glass . . . flowing rhythmically over the court . . . gracefully slicing a deep approach shot into the corner . . . leaping high for an overhead smash . . . deftly angling a backhand volley winner. Aaaaahhhh . . . the daydream.

Your imagination may be the best asset you have. According to several published studies on motor learning, the value of mental practice (thinking about the skill) cannot be underestimated. This is called passive learning — instead of practicing, the student thinks about practicing.

The benefit of mental practice is the student doesn't make errors. Every volley is crisply hit for a winner, every lob hits the baseline, and every drop shot bounces twice inside the service line. This type of practice is good for the ego; it helps develop the student's positive approach to the game.

In his autobiography, Muhammad Ali admitted he couldn't pass a mirror without admiring his style. One quick round of shadow practice and he walked away saying, "Ain't I great!"

And as you think, you are.

All athletes rehearse before going on the court, in the ring, or on the field. They constantly review, analyze and conceptualize. These mental practice sessions are a valuable part of their actual performance. When the time comes to play they've already rehearsed. When the coach tells the player to get "psyched up," he actually is suggesting that he review the game plan, rehearse the skills, get ready to play, etc.

If you are a live-eat-breathe tennis player, nobody needs to tell you to practice mentally — it happens automatically. If, however, you are not yet addicted, maybe a regular planned mental practice session is what you need to get you over the next plateau.

Sit down and close your eyes. Relax all your muscles and picture yourself hitting a smooth, forceful serve deep to the backhand. Now move back quickly and stroke a high arching forehand crosscourt . . .

The only rule of mental practice is to be realistic. Don't waste your time *imagining* shots you have no business trying. Play steady tennis. Always get your first serve in. Don't overhit the ball. Hit only shots you know you can make on the court.

To experiment with passive learning, pick your worst shot and devote a couple minutes twice-a-day to practice. After a week of conscientious *work*, don't be surprised if you notice a marked improvement.

Until then, dream on . . .

Tennis Elbow: How To Prevent And Cure It

Read this. Even though you consider yourself to be indestructable, *tennis elbow* is out there waiting for you to make the wrong move.

First of all, an ache in the elbow means you've done something wrong. Sometimes, all it means is that you've played too much on a certain day, or within a certain period, and your arm rebels by telling you, "Stop! I've had enough!"

To prevent this from happening to you, get the right muscles in shape. (Even if you're a retired blacksmith, TE can put an end to your recreation.) Straighten your arm in front of you with the palm down. Place your non-playing hand on top of your elbow and feel the muscles working as you clench your fist. The muscle on top of the forearm near the elbow is the one to be concerned with; it's called "the backhand muscle." You have to strengthen it.

Take an object weighing about five pounds and hold it at arm's length, palm down. Without bending your elbow, lift it up and down with your wrist until it becomes too heavy. Repeat the exercise a couple times a day, periodically checking its development.

If you already have a case of TE, then start ridding yourself of it. The first step is to place your racquet in a press and put it in the closet; leave it there until your arm gets well.

When you can't feel any pain, buy yourself one of those elbow bands; they seem to help many people ward off further trouble.

Before going back to the courts, and the same style of play that may have caused your problem, have someone qualified look at your strokes. Don't be surprised if they determine the cause of your problem is contacting the ball too late. On the forehand you may roll over the ball on the followthrough, your elbow jutting out like a chicken's wing. This hurts. The undue pressure of the late hit is absorbed by your arm. Practice slowing down all forehand shots, concentrating only on hitting it further in front. Try to keep your elbow down and the racquet pointed straight up in the sky on the followthrough.

The flailing backhand is probably the major cause of tennis elbow. If you don't turn your shoulders and pull the racquet back, you're headed for a late hit. Ouch! Get your shoulders pivoted and the racquet drawn back before the ball clears the net. You'll have a chance to contact the ball in front — the farther in front the better.

Another commonly shared characteristic most *tennis elbow* sufferers share is the sawdust grip. Don't . . . squeeze the racquet, especially after the hit. Relax it in your hand so the grip can breathe. Try taking your hand off the racquet between shots to help save your arm.

The final suggestion may be the toughest to handle: buy a new racquet. It doesn't seem to make much difference what kind, as long as it has a different grip-size and weight. (Some say a slightly larger handle with gut string helps.) The change makes you more conscious of your swing. This extra concentration usually produces a more deliberate swing, and fewer mishits. Whatever the reason, it has helped many others like you.

If all else fails, try copper bracelets, faithhealers, acupuncture and cortisone shots (not necessarily in that order). Hang in there.

How to Warm-up Properly Before Playing

In these frustrating days when it's tough to get a court, and even tougher to stay on, it's important to make every minute count. Pre-play exercises are a great help in saving precious time and, more importantly, prevent athletic injuries. Ideally, the following five exercises should precede your matches.

1) **Stretch your limbs.** The benefit of a three-minute routine of flexing and stretching is invaluable. Without it, your body will take upwards to 20 minutes loosening up.

Find yourself a book on the subject; learn how to stretch the major muscle groups. Memorize a routine so you don't forget an exercise. You'll be surprised how ready you'll be to go all-out on that important first point and game.

2) **Run a little.** It's suggested you walk on the court in a light sweat. Keep your jacket or sweater on during the run and the warmup. Many injuries occur because of a lack of sufficient circulation and body warmth.

3) **Shadow practice.** Before walking on the court, remind your muscles what it feels like to hit all the shots. Walk through your serve, forehand, backhand, approach shots, volleys and overhead. Hit five *pretend* shots of each stroke. Do it in a smooth, slow motion. Watch your racquet as it flows through the backswing, forward swing and followthrough.

4) **Hit against a backboard.** Most facilities have a backboard. Use it! Stand far enough away so the ball will bounce twice to you. Don't bang the ball. Hit high on the board and slowly.

5) **Warm up slowly.** No one is exempt from injury — anybody can get tennis elbow, bursitis, or cartilage problems. Respect your body during the warmup. Even though you prepare properly before walking on the court, don't think you're ready to pull the stops out. Hit your first shots as slowly as possible. Your first few serves should be blooped over the net. Lob your groundstrokes, holding the racquet loose in your hand.

Remember, one of the most depressed human beings is the tennis addict with tennis elbow. Warm up properly!

199

Handicap Your Matches To Make Things Equal

Of all the things contributing to the novice player's frustration with tennis, the number one deterrent is the scoring system. After all, in what other sport can you win a significant number of points and still get beaten 6-0.

It's not fair — especially to the beginner who usually judges himself by the score. Even after losing 6-1 or 6-2, he apologizes to his new tennis partner: "I guess I'm just not enough of a match for you."

So the tennis player is forever on the lookout for someone of equal skill and experience. Winning a 6-4 set is fun, but winning 6-1 is sometimes boring. "Gotta find better matches," he thinks to himself, setting out to find a new opponent.

The end result is that, as you climb the ladder, you find fewer and fewer people to play. Attempting to improve, you ostracize yourself from former tennis-playing friends. This is one of the reasons why many tennis clubs become so *cliquish*. The A players play with the A's, the A-minuses play with the A-minuses, the B players play among themselves, and so on.

To eliminate this snobbish stratification, some clever tennis clubs have found a solution: handicap tournaments. It's the best way to have good competitive fun and keep from losing your precious tennis-playing friends.

There are many ways to handicap tennis matches. Among them are:

1.) Limiting the favorite to only one serve.

2.) Giving the underdog a 15-love lead every game.

3.) Allowing the underdog to hit into the doubles alley.

4.) Giving the underdog a 1, 2 or 3 game lead in each set.

5.) Handicapping the strong serve and volleyer by making it illegal for him to volley the ball until it has bounced once, or twice, on his side.

Probably the best way to handicap a tennis match is via the *Van Allen Simplified Scoring System (VASSS)*. Instead of keeping score of each game (15-30-40, etc.) you keep track of total points, like in ping-pong. The serving rotation is the same also — serve changing sides every five points, players changing sides every ten points. Winner is the first to 31 points with a margin of two.

Playing the system should be mandatory for the player during his first year of play. He should be spared the depressing experience of losing 6-0 for as long as possible.

Try *VASSS* against someone you can handle with ease. Take the difference between the scores and give it to your opponent in a second match. Being down will change the psychological setting of the entire match. It'll do you good.

WHAT TO DO WHEN YOU'RE IN

A SLUMP

There are days when nothing goes the way you plan. This happens to everyone —at every level of play. It's bound to happen to you. Don't become discouraged.

Charting the improvement in your tennis career is much the same as following the performance of an average company on the stock market. There are upward swings of success, plateaus where you remain at the same level, and hard times when you go downhill.

During these hard times try not to get upset with yourself. Think of your poor playing as a bridge that must be crossed before you reach a higher level of play.

Sometimes it's a good idea to stop playing a while when you hit a slump. Your game may be stale for one reason or another and you might need a week or so to get revitalized.

Another suggestion to help motivate you is to watch good tennis. It is both educational and inspirational to watch a championship player in action. It may even help to read a tennis magazine or an instructional book. You may think you know everything about this game, but you'll always find something new and challenging.

Tennis lessons may be what you need to give you a psychological lift. Even if you're satisfied with your strokes, a short lesson on tactics and strategy may help you over the next obstacle.

The final suggestion for breaking out of a slump is simply to work harder. If your forehand is not working, spend time after a match drilling until you're satisfied with the shot. Hit two hundred forehands in succession. If your serve failed you during a match, take a bucket of balls to the court and hit two hundred serves. Take whatever weakness you have and turn it into a strength. This requires hard work.

HOW TO ANTICIPATE BETTER

If you spend a lot of time running one way while the ball goes another, you could benefit from a lesson on anticipation.

The first suggestion is to refrain from admiring your shots.

This is easier said than done. As a beginner you always surprise yourself when the ball goes over the net, and into the court; you just stand there, marveling at the wonder of it all. Later, when you get a little cocky, you start trying for fancy shots in the corners. Since the chances of you hitting it in, and them returning it, are so slim, whenever the two events take place you're caught with your mouth open, out of position.

Players who don't try for so many big winners usually learn to anticipate better — since more of their shots come back.

After you develop the "habit" of expecting a return, it helps to know where it'll go.

In baseline rallies most shots go crosscourt. At the net most passing shots are hit down-the-line.

Inexperienced players share the common problem of not anticipating the short shot. It seems they're always hanging around the baseline when the ball is bouncing inside the service line.

The general rule is to take a step or two inside the court whenever your opponent is: 1) running wide for a ball, 2) playing the ball just after it bounces, while rising, and 3) anytime he's off balance.

You should be able to anticipate a player's return before you hit him the ball (providing you know where you'll hit it). As an example, if you plan to send him a high-bouncing ball to his backhand, get prepared to take a step inside the baseline to anticipate the short underspin return.

Sometimes you fail to reach the ball because your feet get in the way. This can be prevented by moving properly.

Never stop your momentum on the court. Once the point starts keep a steady flow to your footwork.

After hitting the ball, slide, without crossing your feet, back into position. If you're off the court you'll have to run a couple steps, but when your opponent is hitting the ball, slide again.

If you hit a crosscourt groundstroke from the baseline, and anticipate a crosscourt return, bounce lightly on your toes so you'll be "in motion" when he makes contact. If you hit down-the-line, start sliding toward a spot where you anticipate the ball will go — crosscourt.

Now maybe you and the ball will always be going in the same direction.

How to Pick a Tennis Teacher

The more you learn about tennis, the more you find you don't know. That's partly why the game is so addictive.

It is difficult to make headway without proper instruction. For novice players, getting started on the right track is important, especially if the player wants to develop a game that will always develop.

To help insure success it is wise to be selective in choosing an instructor. The range of skill and experience is always great, and if you want to maximize your investment, better do some research.

It may be news to you that there exists a national association of professional tennis teachers. Find out if your proposed teacher is a member of the USPTA. All USPTA members are thoroughly tested before being granted membership. Consult your telephone directory for the number of the local chapter, or ask around.

Call the recreation department, high school or college tennis coach and ask for their suggestions. They'll be glad to give you a reference or two. Or simply go to the courts and ask a few people.

Once you've located two or three well-respected prospects, call them, tell them you want to become a player, and ask if you may watch a couple of their lessons.

After seeing a few lessons you should find it easy to make your choice. You can quickly spot a confident teacher, one who enjoys rapport with his students.

Try not to let the teacher's fee overly influence your decision. You may find quite a range. The "get what you pay for" theory is not always true. The local recreation department may offer excellent instruction, at a real bargain.

After you make your selection and take your first lesson, promise yourself to religiously practice the drills your teacher suggests. Be patient with yourself. Don't expect miracles; in fact, don't expect anything unless you work at it.

How to Teach Your Kids Tennis

If you have a little rug-rat or curtain-climber at home, and you'd like to have him as your doubles partner ten years from now, then read on.

You can introduce tennis to youngsters at an early, early age.

On their first birthday give them a toy racquet or a clean flyswatter. Let them beat it against the furniture.

At the same time fill the house with different sized balls. There are several kinds on the market which are harmless to windows, lamp shades, and antique vases. Put a few in every room and let junior kick and throw them around. (Don't be afraid of stepping on them, because they squish.)

As he, they, or she (especially she) grows up, spend at least a few minutes of every day playing "throw and catch."

The technique of throwing, which is similar to serving, should be taught early. Instruct him to "put the ball in his ear" and let it go. After awhile, ask him to lift his back elbow up to the level of his shoulder before throwing it. "Elbow up, ball in your ear . . . let 'er go."

Periodically challenge the child's throw-ing skills with two tests. In the living room, back yard, or street, keep a mental record of his longest throw.

When he's four, take one of your old racquets, cut the handle down to half length, and re-wrap the grip. Give it to him on a holiday, as a present.

Show him how to hold the racquet in one hand and the ball in the other; then demonstrate how to toss the ball up, let it bounce, then hit it. If he can't do it at first, don't press it.

Continue with the throwing and catching drills, making each day a little more challenging. Toss the balls high and low, slow and fast, until he gradually overcomes his fear of the ball.

To help him learn to catch, show him how to absorb the speed of the ball by bringing his hands into his body as he catches it. (This is an important lesson; it'll prevent him from breaking his thumb at softball games.)

When he's able to bounce the ball repetitively on the ground with his racquet, play "Mini tennis" with him. Practice tapping the ball over a couple trash cans or a rope. Hit to

208

his backhand as often as his forehand.

When he'll practice by himself, encourage him to count his successful hits. Play a game of "See-how-many." How many times can he tap the ball down? Upwards? Across the net? Against the garage?

It is important that as he begins to experience the thrill of controlling the ball you do not discourage him with too many directives. Any technique is okay, as long as he has fun. Be positive and patient.

Even if he never plays at Wimbledon, at least he should have a chance to hold his own in a junior high school P.E. class.

The UNWRITTEN Rules Of Tennis

When first getting started in this game everyone spends too much time apologizing for their lack of skills and ignorance of the rules. When invited to a tennis club they feel conspicuous and uneasy. Mainly, they're afraid of being a nuisance to the veteran tennis buffs playing on adjacent courts.

If this is happening to you, or you know

someone who is presently going through this period, pass on the following *Unwritten Rules of Tennis.*

1.) During the warmup, never say "I'm sorry" after every ball you hit into the net or over the fence . . . Wait until you've hit three in a row, then apologize.

2.) Be accommodating during the warmup. Don't start competing until you keep score.

3.) When you're ready to serve your first game, don't yell out "Love-love, service!" Instead, hold up the balls so he can see you're ready, and say "Play these" . . . or "These go."

4.) Don't wait until you've double-faulted to ask your opponent for "First one in?" Do it beforehand.

5.) On line calls — even though you're not sure if he's sure, don't ask, "Are you sure?" when he calls a close one out.

6.) If your opponent is in a better position to make the call on your side (looking down the line) ask him to make it. If he can't, always assume it was good.

7.) When your opponent is serving, and he double-faults on the first point, don't yell out "Love — 15." Let *him* keep score.

8.) Don't practice your topspin down-the-line returns on his long serves. Even though they're your best shots, it disrupts his concentration. If you accidentally forget, ask him to "take two."

9.) Don't yell "Good get!" until *after* the point is over.

10.) Call set score out before every game (in case you have a slight difference of opinion.)

11.) Graciously give him the point if the ball lands on the outside edge of the line.

12.) Wait until play has stopped to walk behind a court, and to return a ball to the neighboring players. Also, ask players on adjoining courts to return your ball, rather than retrieve it yourself.

13.) Immediately stop the point and "Take two" whenever a ball rolls onto your court.

14.) Benevolently, and with the greatest sincerity, acknowledge all your opponent's exceptional shots (and even the good ones) by saying "Good shot!"

15.) If you win, say nothing; if you lose, no matter for what good reason, say "You were too tough!"

On Cheating, Screaming, and Throwing Your Racquet

Billie Jean King and a thousand football coaches have been quoted as saying, "Show me a good loser and I'll show you a loser."

In tennis, unfortunately, the lousy loser has difficulty finding people to play.

Nobody enjoys seeing a violent display of anger — especially on a tennis court — and especially knowing you caused it.

Yet most of us can't stand losing. It's no fun. And although we don't regularly throw tantrums, everyone goes a little nutsy-whacko once in a while. It's part of the game.

The following practical suggestions probably won't help you become a better loser, but read them anyway.

Before you let out with one of your infamous blood-curdling screams, think about the neighboring players. Someone nearby may be preparing to hit an overhead smash, at the end of a 37-hit rally on the 9th point of a tie-breaker in the third set.

Somehow you've got to let it out without making any noise.

Maybe you could learn how to throw your racquet.

Before you try it, take a moment for a few considerations.

"Let's see . . . If I throw it straight down I'll surely break it . . . If I throw it to my right I could maim the kid on the next court . . . If I throw it to the left that big hulk might get upset and not give it back . . . And if I throw it against the back fence I'll upset the girl behind me concentrating on her serve. So I'll throw it in the net."

"Aaaaaaggggghhhhh!!!!!"

It might be wise to practice throwing your racquet once in awhile. If it's thrown too low you might crack the frame, and if it flies *over* the net it may come back and crack your frame.

As far as technique goes, it seems the most accurate racquet throwers use the Continental Side-Arm style. Hold the racquet at the nob end with three fingers (semi-backhand grip); take it slowly back in a "straight-back" backswing (it's more accurate than the "circular" backswing); point your elbow forward; step toward the net with your left foot on a 45 degree angle; bend your knees (of course); and let 'er go.

If you over-shoot the net it's probably because you lifted your head too soon. Keep your eyes down momentarily (but bring them up soon enough to see the damage you do to the net).

The paradox here is that as your racquet-throwing technique and accuracy improve, so does your tennis playing ability. When you get really good at chucking it into the net, you won't have to anymore.

Regarding your line calls — as much as possible, be objective. Give your opponent the benefit of the doubt. Although many players believe in the motto, "If you're not cheating you're not trying," this will just ruin your social tennis. (When *you're* playing against these "tenacious" competitors there's not much you can do about it, except call an obviously out-ball good — just make sure it's not on game point.)

When you lose, the worst thing you can do is tell him about your planter's wart, your wife's family, your new backhand, or last night's date with your girlfriend's sister. (For a complete list send $10 and a self-addressed, stamped envelope, today.)

Most everyone will forgive a cheatin', screamin', racquet throwin' loser, but nobody likes an obnoxious winner. Instead of saying, "Tough luck, sucker," think of something gracious to say.

213

HOW TO
BE COOL

Are you having trouble picking up matches at the local public courts? Do you stand around all afternoon like a wallflower waiting for someone to walk up and ask you to play? If so, it's probably because you have not figured out how to play the role of the "tennis buff." You're not cool enough.

First of all, consider your apparel. Nobody — I mean nobody — will walk up to you if you're wearing a pair of plaid bermuda shorts and high-top black Converse tennis shoes. Get with it! You must invest in some tennis togs.

Remember though, white is out and color is in. Go for something heavy, like navy blue shorts with a canary yellow shirt. Don't forget to roll your socks down and wear a pair of fancy leather shoes. (Put some *Tennis Goo* on your left toe.)

Now check out your equipment. Better throw away that racquet press or you'll spend your whole career beating your brains out against the backboard. Carry two racquets, preferably wood, in racquet covers. Carry them under your right arm. In the other hand carry a towel and an unopened can of (yellow) tennis balls. (Check around to see what *everyone* is using — it'll only help.)

If you play it right, people will notice you as soon as you show up. Don't exchange their glances. Be cool. Just stand around nonchalantly and watch the match on court No. 1 (it's usually the best tennis). Someone will probably walk up and ask to play.

If you haven't been approached within

five minutes, take your racquet out of its cover and start fiddling with it. Be careful — you must know how to handle the racquet with respect.

Hold it in your right hand at the throat and move the strings around with your left hand. You always see the pros do this, right? It's because the strings get out of place as they brush the ball with topspin.

Now hit the racquet face with the palm of your left hand. Put your ear next to the racquet and listen for the ping of your gut (naturally) strings. You're checking the tension of the strings.

If you've followed directions carefully, you should have a match by now. Don't blow your cool yet. If you do, your new partner just might happen to notice that his match showed up.

As you get to the court, lay your extra racquet against the net and quickly open your can of balls. Accidentally drop one of the balls on the court. After it stops bouncing, take your racquet and tap it hard, contacting it at the top of the frame with the racquet at a 45-degree angle to the ground. Hit it hard once and pull the racquet away. It should bounce up to you. If you succeed — congratulations! This is the biggest psych job in the world. He's apt to be impressed.

Now spin the racquet on the ground and simultaneously say, "M or W?" If he picks "M," then casually glance at the butt of the racquet and say, "It's W . . . I'll serve." (If the racquet doesn't have an "M" or a "W," do it anyway; they'll never question you.)

Don't let him warm up. If he sees how bad you are, he'll think of an excuse not to play. Tell him you like to warm up slowly as you play. Once you serve, he'll have to finish at least a set. Otherwise, you win by default.

Stand as close to the center service mark as possible. (That's the little line in the middle of the long line at the end of the court.) Hold one ball up for him to see (put the other one in your left pocket). This means that you are ready to play. Do not play "first one in." That is definitely uncool.

Bounce the ball a few times. Now look across the net and dribble it a few more times. Look again and bounce it down once more. (Don't bounce it off your foot!)

Toss it up slowly and hit it . . . "Fault!" Whatever you think, never question his call. Take the second one out and go through the same bouncing routine. Toss it up and try it again — "Double fault!"

Oh well.

A Summary

- The objective of the serve is to start the point — not to finish it.
- The #1 tactic: Hit the ball over the net. Play mountain tennis.
- Anatomically, the underspin backhand is an easier shot to hit.
- Try to be selective when spectating; learn by watching good players.
- Repetition is learning.
- Your goal is to make positive errors; instead of brooding over an error, learn from it.
- Count your hits; when you can average three per point, consider yourself a steady, mature tennis player.
- Say ERP . . . BOUNCE . . . and ARMPIT.
- Before you can learn to hit the ball hard, first learn to hit softly.
- Your improper technique is responsible for some errors, but the great majority result from either excess speed or too much angle.
- If you respect its difficulty, tennis is an easy game to learn.
- A quiet body at the point of contact makes this game a cinch.
- Hold your finish until the ball bounces on the other side of the net; the followthrough position indicates what took place during the stroke.
- Pretend you have numbers on the back of your shirt, like a baseball player; whenever a ball approaches your backhand side, rotate your shoulders so your opponent can see your numbers.
- The sorriest victim is the guy who momentarily loses his head, lobs, and rushes the net.
- After playing shortcourt, moving back to the baseline, you'll experience a spacious freedom you never knew existed.

216

9¢
STAMP

Please send me _____ copies of WATCH THE BALL, BEND YOUR KNEES, THAT'LL BE $20 PLEASE! I enclose $5.95 per copy plus 75¢ per order for postage and handling.

Amount of order $_____.

Charge to ☐ Bank Americard (VISA)   ☐ Master Charge

Card No. _____ Exp. Date_____

Name _____

Address _____

City _____ State _____ Zip _____

Caroline House Books
236 Forest Park Place
Ottawa, Illinois 61350

9¢
STAMP

Please send me _____ copies of WATCH THE BALL, BEND YOUR KNEES, THAT'LL BE $20 PLEASE! I enclose $5.95 per copy plus 75¢ per order for postage and handling.

Amount of order $_____.

Charge to ☐ Bank Americard (VISA)   ☐ Master Charge

Card No. _____ Exp. Date_____

Name _____

Address _____

City _____ State _____ Zip _____

Caroline House Books
236 Forest Park Place
Ottawa, Illinois 61350

9¢
STAMP

Please send me _____ copies of WATCH THE BALL, BEND YOUR KNEES, THAT'LL BE $20 PLEASE! I enclose $5.95 per copy plus 75¢ per order for postage and handling.

Amount of order $_____.

Charge to ☐ Bank Americard (VISA)   ☐ Master Charge

Card No. _____ Exp. Date_____

Name _____

Address _____

City _____ State _____ Zip _____

Caroline House Books
236 Forest Park Place
Ottawa, Illinois 61350

9¢
STAMP

Please send me _____ copies of WATCH THE BALL, BEND YOUR KNEES, THAT'LL BE $20 PLEASE! I enclose $5.95 per copy plus 75¢ per order for postage and handling.

Amount of order $_____.

Charge to ☐ Bank Americard (VISA)   ☐ Master Charge

Card No. _____ Exp. Date_____

Name _____

Address _____

City _____ State _____ Zip _____

Caroline House Books
236 Forest Park Place
Ottawa, Illinois 61350

9¢
STAMP

Please send me _____ copies of WATCH THE BALL, BEND YOUR KNEES, THAT'LL BE $20 PLEASE! I enclose $5.95 per copy plus 75¢ per order for postage and handling.

Amount of order $_____.

Charge to ☐ Bank Americard (VISA)   ☐ Master Charge

Card No. _____ Exp. Date_____

Name _____

Address _____

City _____ State _____ Zip _____

Caroline House Books
236 Forest Park Place
Ottawa, Illinois 61350

9¢
STAMP

Please send me _____ copies of WATCH THE BALL, BEND YOUR KNEES, THAT'LL BE $20 PLEASE! I enclose $5.95 per copy plus 75¢ per order for postage and handling.

Amount of order $_____.

Charge to ☐ Bank Americard (VISA)   ☐ Master Charge

Card No. _____ Exp. Date_____

Name _____

Address _____

City _____ State _____ Zip _____

Caroline House Books
236 Forest Park Place
Ottawa, Illinois 61350

Please send me _____ copies of WATCH THE BALL,
BEND YOUR KNEES, THAT'LL BE $20 PLEASE! I enclose
$5.95 per copy plus 75¢ per order for postage and handling.

Amount of order $_____.

Charge to ☐ Bank Americard (VISA)   ☐ Master Charge

Card No. _____ Exp. Date_____

Name _____

Address _____

City _____ State _____ Zip _____

Caroline House Books
236 Forest Park Place
Ottawa, Illinois 61350

Please send me _____ copies of WATCH THE BALL,
BEND YOUR KNEES, THAT'LL BE $20 PLEASE! I enclose
$5.95 per copy plus 75¢ per order for postage and handling.

Amount of order $_____.

Charge to ☐ Bank Americard (VISA)   ☐ Master Charge

Card No. _____ Exp. Date_____

Name _____

Address _____

City _____ State _____ Zip _____

Caroline House Books
236 Forest Park Place
Ottawa, Illinois 61350